Artistica[illegible]
Cultivated [illegible]os

To Valerie et al
Love from
The Glidden
gang
Christmas 2016

Elise Felton is an experienced horticulturist and winner of numerous "best in show" garden and flower show awards. She is well known for her successful propagation and growing of interesting plants. Her practical experience can help you to enjoy success in growing your favorite herbs in pleasing designs.

Artistically Cultivated Herbs

How to Train Herbs as Decorative Art

By Elise Felton

Illustrated by Hilda Wilson Bourgeois

Woodbridge Press

Santa Barbara, California 93160

1992

Published by

Woodbridge Press Publishing Company
Post Office Box 6189
Santa Barbara, California 93160

Printed in the United States of America
Distributed simultaneously in Canada

Library of Congress Cataloging in Publication Data

Felton, Elise.
Artistically cultivated herbs.
Includes bibliographical references.
1. Herb gardening. 2. Plants—training. I. Title.
SB351.H5F435 1990 635'.7 90-12316
ISBN 0-88007-180-X

Trade Names

Certain trade names are mentioned in this book solely as a convenience to readers; the author has no connection with the companies concerned. The following trade names are trademarks of the companies indicated.

Beetle Trap Attack—Reuter, Dallas, Texas.
Metromix—Grace Horticultural Products, Cambridge, Massachusetts.
Peters Soluble Plant Food, *Peters Professional* Potting Soil, Peters Co., Allentown, Pennsylvania.
Safer—Safer, Inc., Newton, Massachusetts.
Sunshine—Fisions Horticulture, Inc., Vancouver, British Columbia.
SuperSorb—Aquatrols Corp. of America. Pennsauken, New Jersey.
Terra-Green—OilDri, Chicago, Illinois.
Twist-ems—Germain's, Inc., Los Angeles, Califiornia.
Water Grabber—F.P. Products, Lake City, South Carolina.

Cover illustrations: Janice Blair

Page layout: Lily Guild

To Jean Whitton Haskin
whose wit, intelligence, enthusiasm,
and elegant style
all combined in her love of herbs.

Acknowledgements

To my husband, Sam Felton, goes great appreciation for his enthusiastic encouragement and the use of his time, not only to house this book on his PC, but also for his ideas and his practical approaches to crafting a book.

I wish to thank Cecily Clark and Susan Moody for going over the manuscript with a fine-toothed comb and making many valuable corrections. Cecily, an old hand at editing and a superb, meticulous grower, took the creases out of my awkward English. Susan, an herbal horticulturist, did not hesitate to write in the manuscript margins, "Don't understand," thereby helping me to clarify points.

Fine comments and suggestions came from a number of horticultural experts: Thomas DeBaggio, Madalene Hill, Barbara Luplow, Sally MacBride, Holly Shimizu, and Ivan Watters, all of whom read the entire manuscript. Ivan had much input on the bonsai chapter.

Arthur O. Tucker, of Delaware State College, was a big help with herbal nomenclature, an area I find very time consuming and frustrating.

Galen Gates and Hans Zutter added meaty horticultural tips, and Heidi Randen typed the entire manuscript.

Lastly, much appreciation to Hilda Wilson Bourgeois Daly for her wonderful drawings that enliven and give clarity to the text.

Contents

Introduction

This book has been written for everyone who loves plants and enjoys working with them in a direct and artistic way.

How I wish I could have had such a book ten years ago. Instead, I travelled through much uncharted territory, learning largely through trial and error. Thus, I hope this book will help you to benefit from that experience and to quickly apply a set of simple, practical procedures to enhance your pleasure in herbal horticulture.

Although procedures described here deal with herbs, they can be applied to other plants, as with standards that may be created with coleus, eye-catching strawberry jars of succulents, or tied topiaries using English ivy.

These procedures are also applicable to a wide range of growing conditions: in the East, where I am from originally, or in the Midwest, Southwest, Southern California, the Pacific Northwest, or in Canada—the advice is applicable virtually everywhere.

Not only will these procedures provide a pleasant outlet for creativity—the planting, snipping, grooming, and watering are also a relaxing therapy. One moves slowly and gently, for plants respond to kindly nurturing. Creating horticultural beauty is very satisfying.

I have been mindful of the smaller spaces in which many of us are housed these days; this book should be useful to those who garden in containers occupying small spaces as well as to those who have more room.

Jean Haskin, to whose memory this book is dedicated, introduced me to herbs, thereby broadening my own herbal horizons. Together we watched herbs grow, often surprised with the unexpected. She would have liked this book, written and illustrated by two of her good friends.

Working with specimen herbs has been most rewarding to me. I hope this book will encourage you to try these new ways of growing herbs . . . ways that will result in beautiful plants and a more beautiful and pleasant environment for you and your family.

CHAPTER 1

The Secrets of Growing

GROWING HERBS is fun and it is richly rewarding. Herbs ask so little and give so much. Not only are herbs lovely to look at, they are rewarding to touch or brush in passing. The deliciously scented oils stored in their leaves are a sensual delight.

Three Important Elements

THERE ARE THREE important elements that must be considered in order to grow herbs successfully: light, temperature, and soil.

Light

Most herbs need sunny growing conditions—at least five hours of sun a day; or, in winter, sixteen hours under flourescent lights placed about two to four inches above the plants. (One cool-white and one warm-white bulb in a two-bulb fixture should work well.) It is light that develops essential oils in the leaves—the ingredient used in cooking or in making fragrances or medicines.

A rule of thumb: the darker the leaf the less light the plant will need. Variegated and silver-toned plants need long hours of bright light (but less water than green plants) because their leaves contain less chlorophyll, the green pigment with which light reacts in the process of photosynthesis.

Temperature

Ideally, herbs should grow outside where they will have all of the best conditions: heat, light, rain, humidity, and moving air. In colder climes they will need protection, with ideal winter temperatures of 65°F or more by day and 55°F or more at night.

Soil

Herbs require well-drained soil. With the exception of the mints they will not tolerate "wet feet." For container growing, try using the growing mix, Metromix #350 or #360, produced by the Grace Company. This soilless mix encourages the development of wonderful root systems. It contains processed bark ash, a charcoalated pine bark that provides air spaces so roots can absorb oxygen. Charcoal particles have sharp edges as do many other solid particles, like small stones. Feeder roots will divide when they come up against these edges. The multiplication of feeder roots provides the plant with more roots which will, in turn, supply the plant with more oxygen, water, and mineral salts.

This mix also contains sphagnum peat (organic material), vermiculite, sand, and nutrients. If it is not available, one can substitute Peter's Professional Potting Soil, a similar mixture. Sunshine All-Purpose Potting Mix can also be used, but it does not contain processed bark ash. All of these mixes also contain a soil wetting agent that improves the ability of water to penetrate the growing media. These soilless mixes are recommended for container growing, although well-drained, natural soil will also keep herbs safe from rot during periods of extended rainfall and from overzealous watering.

To make a soil drain faster, one can add perlite, grit, or Torpedo Sand (grade #FA2), all of which are nonporous and shed water, creating air pockets. Another soil additive is Terra-Green Soil-Conditioner. Its granules are noncompacting and nondecomposing. It aids in keeping soil loose, thereby increasing air spaces for the roots to take in oxygen and release carbon dioxide.

The most important addition to waterlogged soil is organic material, such as peat moss, compost, or leaf mold, to aid drainage, to promote aeration, and to hold onto moisture and nutrients. Organic material also improves microflora and microfauna, and minimizes the fluctuation of soil temperature.

The Mediterranean coastline herbs—rosemary, sages and thymes, savories and lavenders—are most particular about well-drained soil. The Umbelliferae family of herbs, like parsley and coriander, and the mint family, Labitae, prefer a richer soil containing more compost or loam.

Polymers, which look like small chips, increase the water-holding capacity of soils and soil mixes by holding water in "chunks." without loss of air space. With increased moisture reserves, more water is available longer for plant roots. But remember that soil media in containers will expand 15 to 20 percent when watered. So if one uses polymers when planting herbs in containers, he should lower the soil level accordingly. Polymers are available at garden centers and can be mixed into the planting soil in the proportion, in relation to the soil, indicated on the label. Two of the trade names are Water Grabber and SuperSorb C.

Suggested Proportions of Polymers to Soil

If the label says to mix: 1½ *lbs.* polymers per cubic *yard* of soil, you may use 1 to 3 *oz.* polymers per cubic *foot* of soil.

A cubic foot of soil is one foot square by one foot high. Four 12-inch hanging baskets will hold about one cubic foot of soil.

Soilless Mixes

Metromix #350 and #360

Canadian sphagnum peat moss
Domestic horticultural vermiculite
Horticultural perlite
Processed bark ash (a patented process)
Washed granite sand
Wetting agent
Nutrient charge (lasts seven to ten days)

Peters Professional Potting Soil

Canadian sphagnum peat moss
Horticultural vermiculite
Processed bark ash (a patented process)
Sometimes, sand
Wetting agent
Nutrient charge (lasts seven to ten days)

Sunshine All-Purpose Potting Mix

Canadian sphagnum peat moss
Vermiculite
Perlite
Dolomitic limestone
Charcoal
Wetting agent

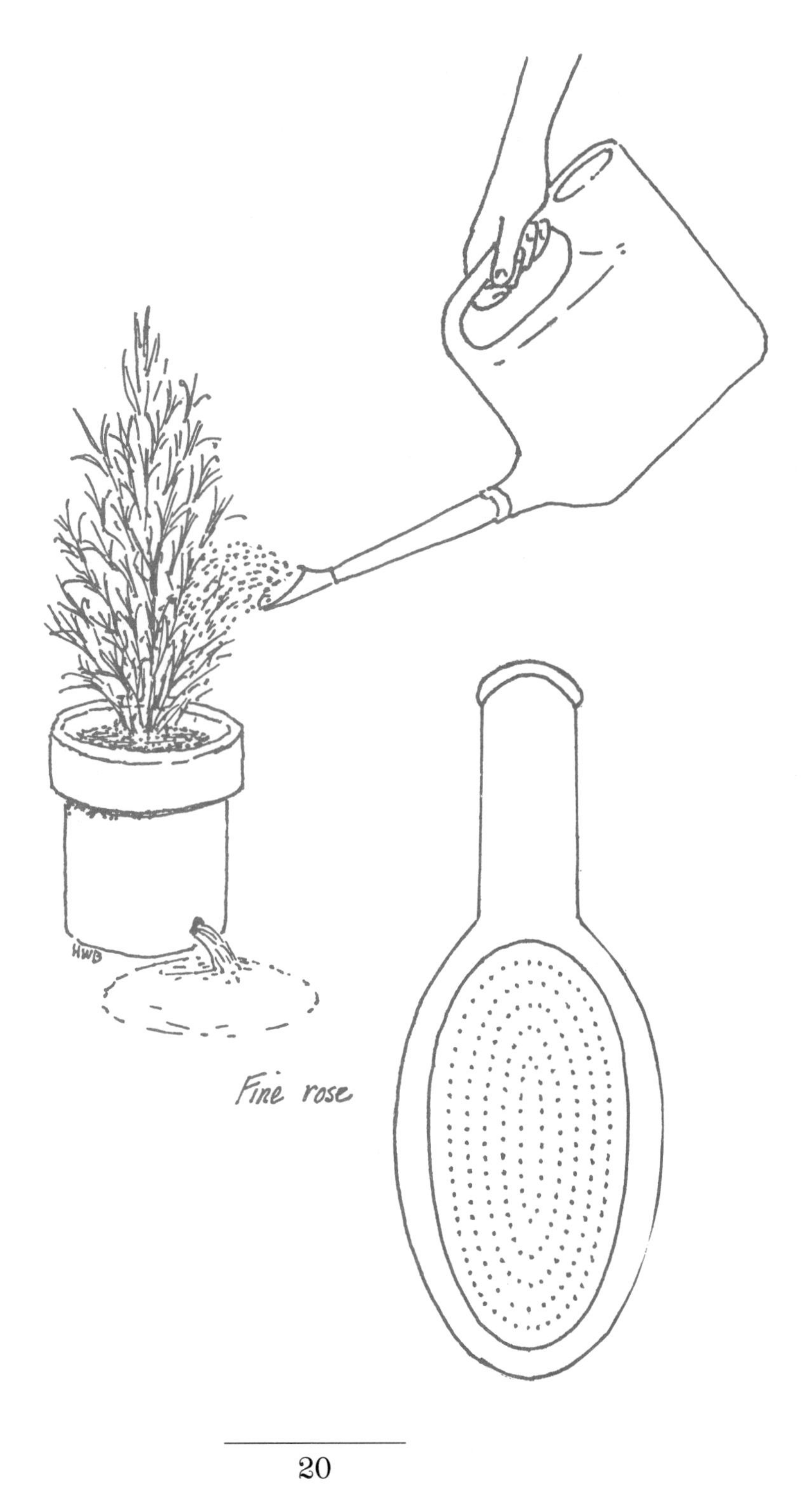
HWB
Fine rose

Water

CONTAINER-GROWN plants must be watered when dry, although herbs tolerate a dryer soil than do many other plants. Many of them come from the Mediterranean region where the summers are dry, the days warm and sunny, and the soil rocky, with little humus to retain moisture.

A rule of thumb: the thinner the leaf, the more water the plant will need. There are those who say this is a myth, but it works for me!

Here is an easy way to test a container-grown plant for dryness: keep a plastic plant label inserted between the soil and the side of the container. If soil sticks to the label when it is pulled out, the plant does not need watering. Garden-planted herbs can send their roots down into the soil to search for moisture, but potted ones are restricted and in dry periods may need watering as often as twice a day.

Young annual herbs will require more water than established perennial herbs because they are growing rapidly. Containers of perennial herbs can be allowed to dry out between waterings, but the smaller the container the more watering it will require. Other dehydrating factors are very hot sun, dry wind, and high temperatures.

The Umbelliferae (carrot family) and Labiatae (mint family) prefer more water. Some mints, such as the peppermints and spearmints, can tolerate damp conditions.

When watering herbs, use a wand on the end of a hose, or a bonsai nozzle, to create a very fine stream of water. If a watering can is used, be sure to use a fine "rose" on the spout. Except in the heat of summer, I water all my plants with warm (to touch) water, about 92°F.

It is always best to water early in the day so the plants will have a reserve for photosynthesis, a daytime process. A plant's need for water depends on air temperatures, the amount of sunshine, the day-length, the strength of the winds, the container size and construction (plastic or clay), and the plant's special preference.

The dropping of inner leaves that have turned brown on the Mediterranean herbs indicates that there is too much water in the soil. Yellow leaves can be a sign of a lack of nutrients or that the plant is rootbound. Understanding the needs of plants can be difficult—watering is an art.

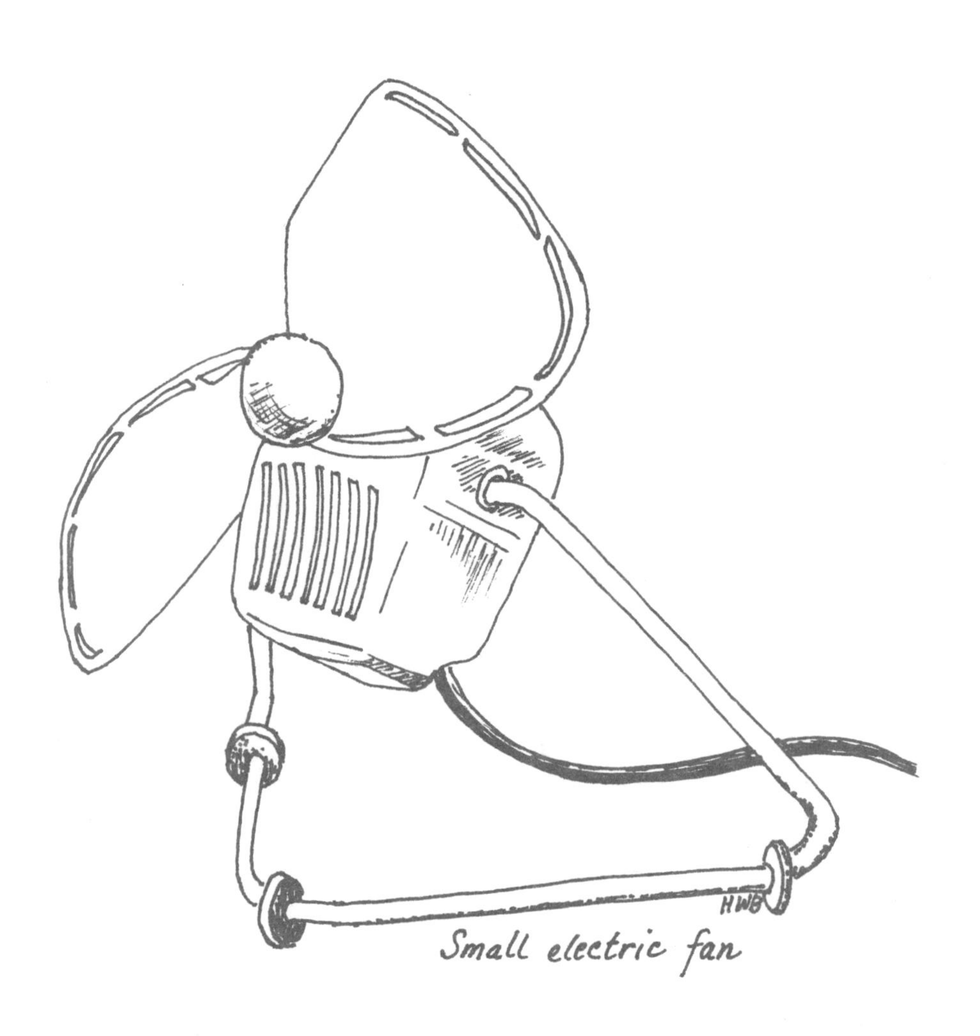

Small electric fan

Air Circulation

PROPER AIR CIRCULATION is important. In container-growing outdoors, air circulation can be controlled by leaving walking room between the containers. Indoors, or in a greenhouse, fans should be used to keep the air moving. Small plastic fans, such as one manufactured by Caframo, with uncaged blades, are readily available and relatively safe. If you accidentally run into one, you will not be hurt—just surprised.

Fertilizing

THE NEED for fertilizers—those elements from which green plants manufacture their own food—depends on the soil mixture. Commercial soil mixes sometimes have fertilizer additives that will be washed away by watering. There are two alternatives: place a slow-release fertilizer on top of the soil ball or use a soluble fertilizer according to directions on the label. Sometimes both methods are used at the same time.

I use Peters 20-20-20 (equal parts of nitrogen, phosphorous, and potassium) dissolved in a watering can. The warmer the atmosphere, the more watering the plants will need and the more nutrients will be leached out of the soil. Therefore, I fertilize more often during hot, sunny days and not at all during the winter when the plants are not making new growth.

Fertilizing herbs can cut down on their oil production—and one of the reasons for growing herbs is the appealing odors and tastes that are in those volatile oils. My main objective, however, is horticultural perfection—a balance between fragrant leaves and artistic form (T. DeBaggio Herbs recommends 20-10-20 for fertilizing herbs.)

Three Main Minerals

Here is a *quick review* of the *three main minerals* we use for fertilizer:

• *Nitrogen* gives foliage a true greenness and encourages rich growth.

• *Phosphorous* is necessary for flowering and fruit set, and it encourages good root growth.

• *Potassium* is responsible for general hardiness, resistance to disease, and plant vigor.

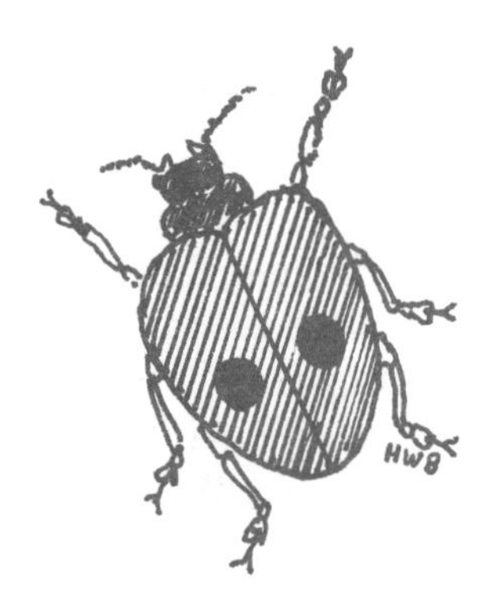

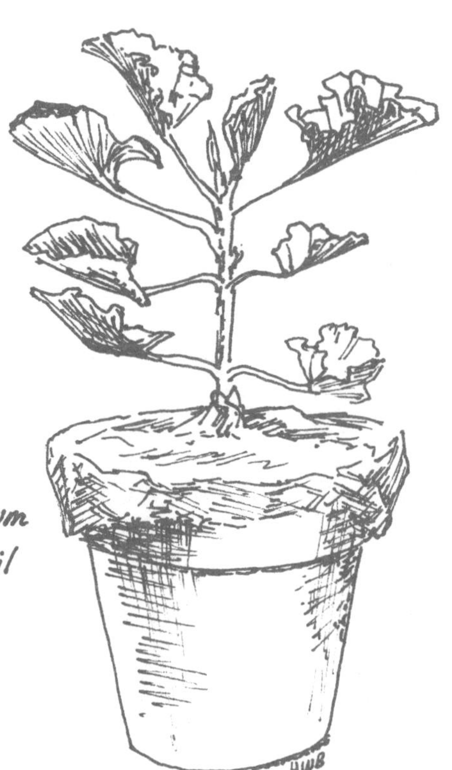

Cover top of pot with aluminum foil to keep soil from splashing

Insects and Diseases

INSECTS AND DISEASES rarely bother herbs grown outside. Greenhouse-grown herbs are more susceptible to infestations. Indoors or out, aphids sometimes appear at the growing tips. A spray of Safer's Insecticidal Soap will do away with them. If plants are outside, lady beetles will feast on the aphids. Lady beetles can be purchased at some garden shops or by mail or UPS for use either in the greenhouse or outdoors. White fly on lemon verbena can be a problem. Try Safer's Soap every third day, but do not spray in full sun as there is risk of burning the foliage—and be sure to also spray the undersides of the leaves.

In the Northeast, Japanese beetles can plague basil. Beetles can be hand picked in the early morning. Commercial traps are available, such as Beetle Trap Attack or Safer's Disposable Trap. Beetles are lured into the traps with floral and sex pheromone lures. Remember to change the collecting bag every day.

Powdery mildew can be a nasty happening on certain rosemarys in a cool greenhouse. Either throw away the affected plants and grow a more fungus-resistant variety or use a fungicidal spray, such as Safer's Garden Fungicide, which can be "used until the day of harvest," according to the manufacturer.

Another alternative is to spray rosemary plants with Wilt-Pruf, an antitranspirant, when they are brought indoors. This will protect the leaves from powdery mildew. The spraying may have to be repeated.

Scale is likely to appear on the leaves and stems of bay. Eliminate these with cotton balls soaked in rubbing alcohol. It's fun if you can recruit a friend to share in this chore—one on each side of the plant, working from the bottom up while turning the plant clockwise, can make short work of it, or try Safer's Insecticidal Soap.

Safer has 84 such products on the market. They contain fatty acids and potassium salts, which are natural biopesticides. The manufacturer states that their products are safe when used as directed and do not affect honey bees or lady beetles. You can call their lab with questions at 1-800-544-4453.

To prevent insects from invading indoor plants, it is wise to give the plants a weekly spraying with water. Wrap aluminum foil around the top of the container to cover the soil and prevent splashing, and place the plant in a shower or under a sprayer in the kitchen sink. If we dust our

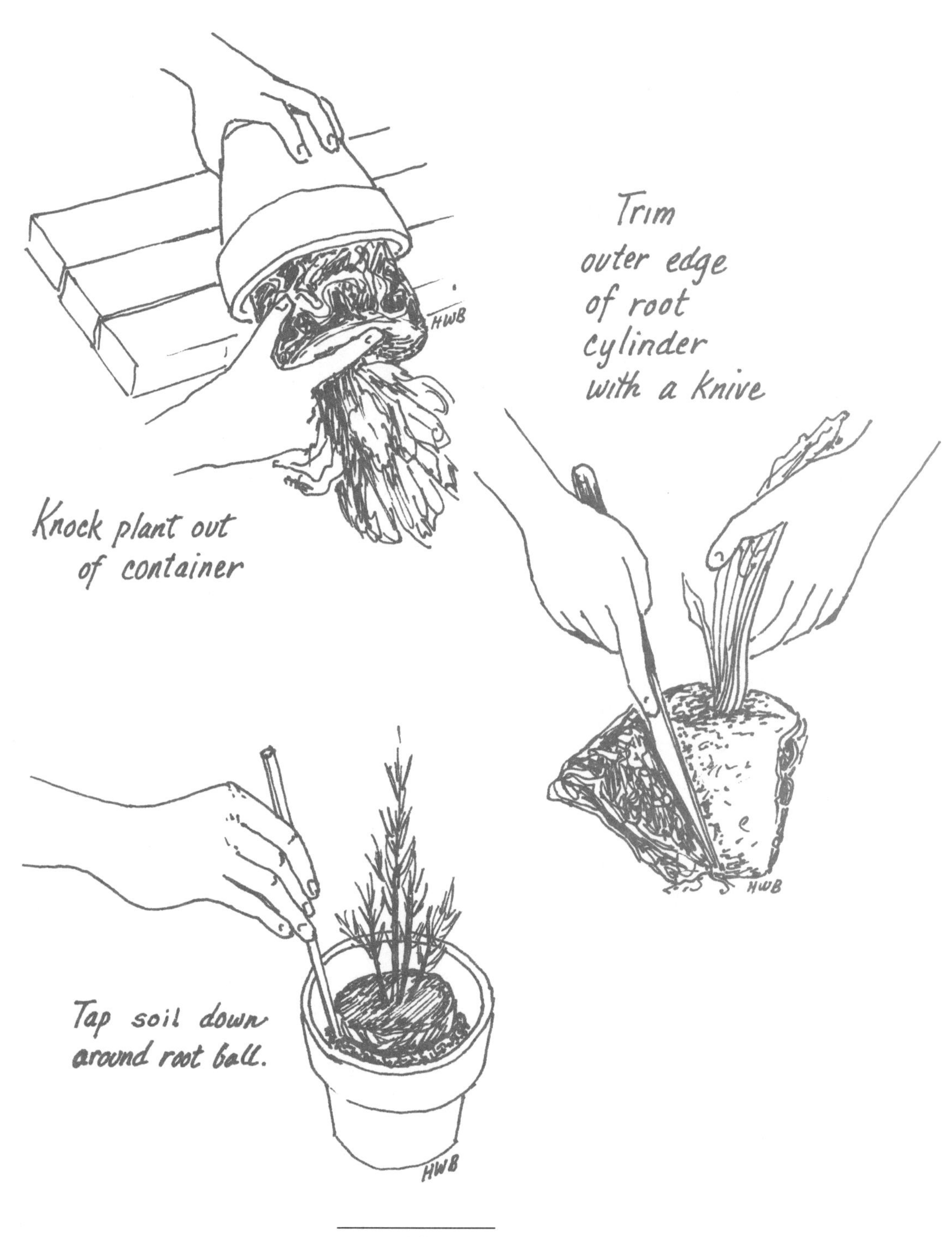
Trim
outer edge
of root
cylinder
with a knive
Knock plant out
of container
Tap soil down
around root ball.

houses once a week, shouldn't we give our plants equal attention? A "mister" attached to the greenhouse hose does the job easily.

A moist microclimate is the best prevention against a spider mite invasion. They like hot and dry conditions. Safer's Insecticidal Soap will help to control an infestation.

Repotting

REPOTTING is essential for herbs as they produce large root systems. If a potted herb is dry and needs to be watered constantly, it is an indication that the container has filled up with roots. Roots need oxygen and moisture and can get both only when there are spaces between soil particles. The plant cannot live when these spaces are filled. Organic material in the soil is what holds onto moisture, and a root-bound plant has little access to this organic material.

To repot, knock the plant out of its container to see how dense the root system is. If there is a thick mass of roots, the plant needs root pruning and repotting. Early spring is a good time to repot when the plant is starting a period of active growth and requires space to produce new roots and foliage. In the case of herbs trained as bonsai, where the rootball is necessarily meagre, it is important to top prune the plant to compensate for root reduction.

To root-prune, cut about an inch* of the roots off the root ball all the way around with sharp scissors or a knife. (Black roots are dead and will slough off. White roots are alive and should be lightly pruned.) Then cut a layer off the bottom. The root ball will then be reduced by about *one third.* Decide if the plant should be repotted in a one-size larger container or if it can remain in the same size pot. Always use a fresh, clean container. Place a piece of plastic wire mesh (fiberglass insect cloth) over the drainage hole of the container to keep the soil from running out of the bottom. Then place fresh soil on the bottom, replace the pruned root ball, and add soil all around, making sure that the plant is centered and that the soil level is the same as it was before. Use the eraser end of a pencil or a chopstick to tamp the soil down between the root ball and the sides of the container. Do not ever press on the root ball itself.

*More or less, depending on the diameter at the root ball.

Correct pruning cut
Select bud pointing direction new growth should go.
Cut just above the bud, using clean, sharp pruning shears, on a 45° angle that starts from just above the bud and ends level with the base of the bud.
Cut too steep Too much heartwood exposed
Cut too far from bud - will not heal
Cut too close to bud - bud may dry up.
HWB
Incorrect pruning cuts

Repotted plants must be watered immediately. Place them in a tub or sink of tepid water up to the rim of the pots. In this way moisture is soaked up through the drainage hole and the soil drops down around the roots, preventing the possibility of air pockets forming around the roots.

Herbs acquired from a commercial grower—purchased in pots, pans, or packs—will most likely have matted, white root systems. Before replanting them in the garden or in containers, their root balls should be broken up by hand or cut or scored with a knife on the bottom and on all four sides. This procedure will encourage the growth of new roots.

Pruning and Harvesting

PRUNING RULES are the same for all plants. First remove all the dead branches, including any stubs. Then cut the branches back to just above a live bud—at an angle. Choose a bud facing the direction of a wanted branch. Next remove any branches growing toward the center of the plant. Then prune for shape.

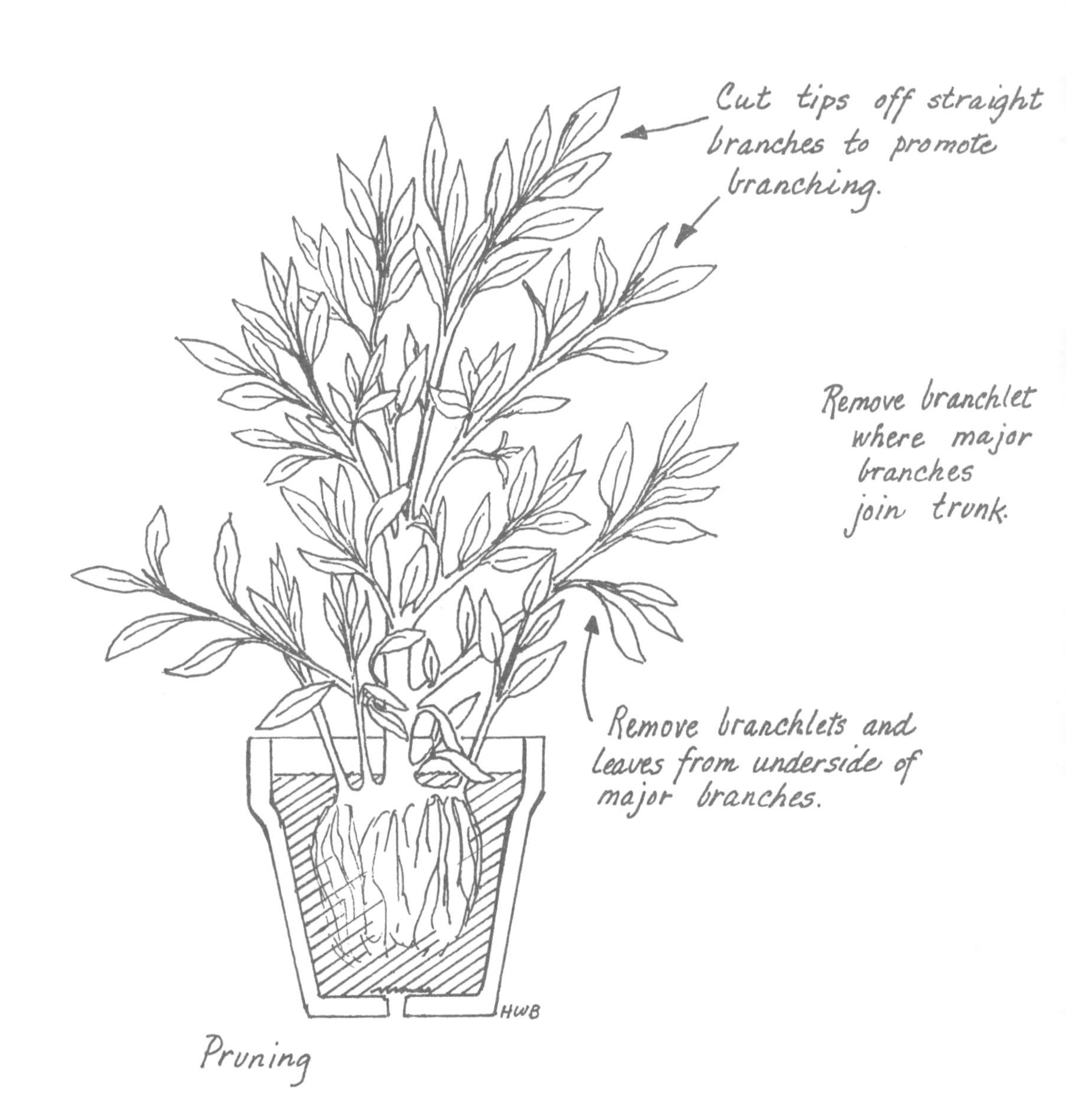
Cut tips off straight branches to promote branching.
Remove branchlet where major branches join trunk.
Remove branchlets and leaves from underside of major branches.
HWB
Pruning

Laurus nobilis

Allow eye to see sculptural form of the plant.

H.W.B.

With ornamental woody herbs, such as bays *(Laurus nobilis)* and rosemaries (*Rosmarinus* spp.), cut away all the superfluous growth along the branches, allowing the eye to see the sculptural form of the plant to best advantage. (This might result in removing branchlets where major branches join the trunk.) Also remove the branchlets and leaves from the undersides of major branches. Always remove any crossing branches. Work with what is left to achieve a pleasing form with a view to having the new growth going upward and outward.

Take the time to harvest herbs. While snipping and pruning can be done anytime, herbs will have more flavor when harvested in summer. Rules for harvesting and preserving herbs are thoroughly covered in *Southern Herb Growing,* by Madalene Hill and Gwen Barclay with Jean Hardy (Fredericksburg, TX: Shearer Publishing, 1987). The best time to harvest is midmorning after the sun has dried the leaves.

Do not leave stubs when harvesting parsley and chives. Cut the leaves and stalks down to the soil level. This procedure will give the plant a neater and more attractive appearance.

Pot Rotation

FOR SYMMETRICAL GROWTH, it is important to rotate all plants, particularly those situated on a winter windowsill where the sun enters at a low angle. During the hot growing season, rotate plants clockwise a quarter turn twice a week. While caddies supporting heavy plants can be used, the plastic wheels can be difficult to rotate if the caddies are outdoors. Homemade dollies with rubber wheels with ball bearings are much easier to move with heavy plants on board.

Which Pot?

CHOOSING A SUITABLE container for herbs deserves careful consideration. With a large collection of container-grown plants, the effect will be more harmonious if they are grown in pots made of similar materials. If the choice is plastic, make sure that the pots are all the same color. Green is my preference.

Plastic pots are nonporous and do not allow for the proper circulation of air and moisture as do clay pots. Although cheaper and lighter, plastic

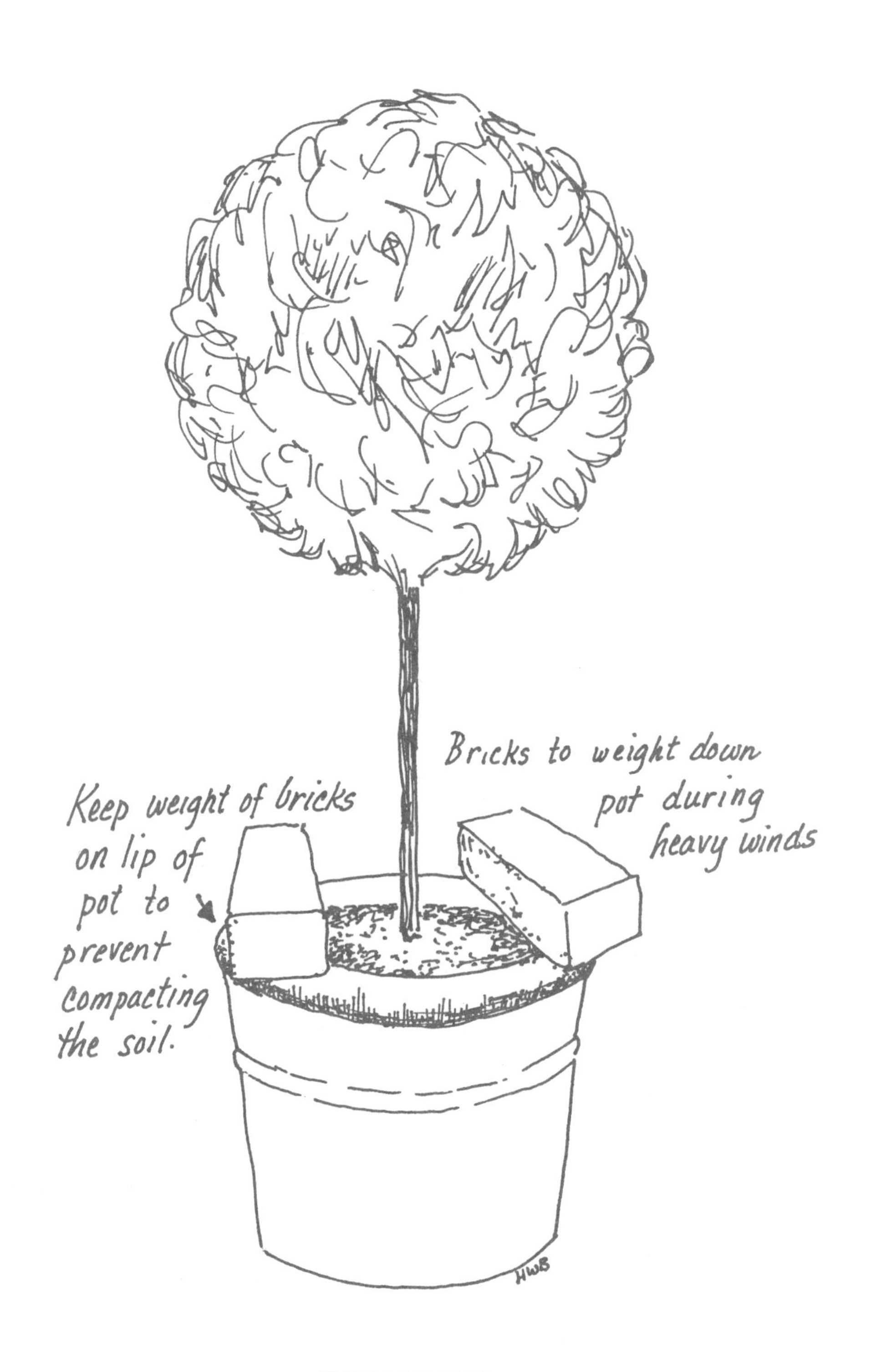
Keep weight of bricks
on lip of
pot to
prevent
compacting
the soil.
Bricks to weight down
pot during
heavy winds
HWB

containers are unstable in a windy location, and are not permitted in some flower shows. However, accumulated salts are not as difficult to remove from plastic, and the fact that plastic retains moisture in the soil can help to reduce the amount of watering needed.

Clay pots are heavier, break easily, and are more expensive than plastic containers. Moisture evaporates through their porous walls, leaving a collection of salts on their rims and down their sides. Herbs grown in clay pots will need three times more watering than those in plastic pots. The heavy waterer will do best with clay pots as the odds of drowning herbs is greatly reduced. Despite the problems clay pots present, on the whole they are a better choice as containers, both culturally and aesthetically.

Clay pots come in the following standard sizes (according to diameter in inches at the top): 2½, 3, 4, 5, 6, 7, 8, 9, 10, 12, 14, 16, and 18 inches.

Resist the temptation to use highly ornamented "designer pots." The ornamentation tends to overpower a well-grown plant that would otherwise stand on its own. Decorative pots can also detract from foilage texture and plant form. Most of them are fired at very high temperatures, eliminating porosity and thereby holding too much water for good herb cultivation.

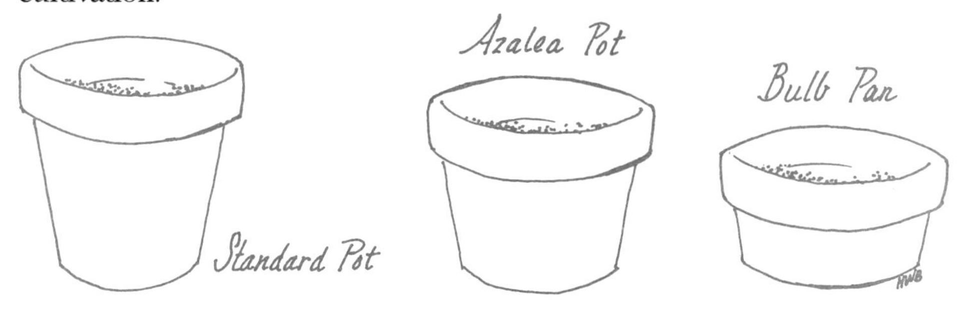

Wind and Storms

COPING WITH WIND is a big challenge for the container grower when plants are grown outdoors. Storms, tornados, and other vagaries of nature require instant action. I keep a pile of heavy paving bricks nearby, and the minute the wind picks up I dash around placing bricks on the tops of the larger containers. The smaller ones I either bring under shelter or surround with bricks to prevent their toppling over. A top

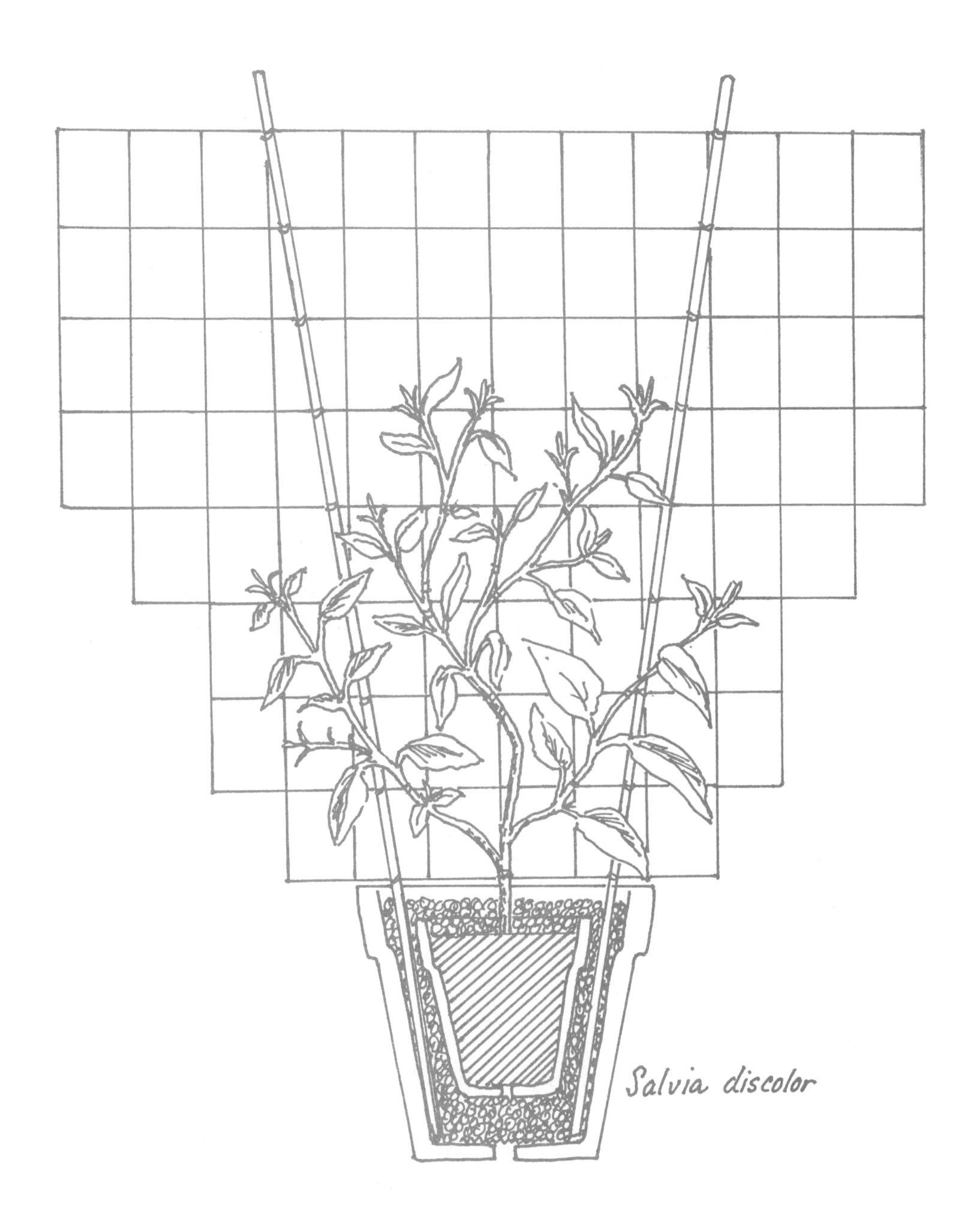
Salvia discolor

dressing of pebbles adds weight to the containers and conserves moisture when plants are outdoors, or one might try using square-based containers as they rarely blow over. Placing plants in an area protected from the wind is optimal. However, be sure that the plants receive at least five hours of sun a day as well as the proper air circulation.

I recommend double potting top-heavy plants, such as standards. To do this, take a pot at least two inches larger in diameter, place a piece of wire mesh over the drainage hole, and pour in an inch or two of pea gravel (pebbles). Then place the standard, pot and all, inside the second pot and fill the sides with pebbles, spreading them over both the soil surface and the lip of the inside pot. This is a particularly practical way of coping with container-grown vines on trellises.

Sand in Saucers and Pans

IF POTS OF HERBS are situated on a hot surface such as cement or brick, the containers should be set in clay saucers filled with sand in order to stabilize the plants and provide cool pads for the roots. Drainage holes should be drilled in either clay or plastic saucers, using a masonry bit on an electric drill. Cover the holes with plastic wire mesh and fill the saucers halfway with sand.

In the warmer weather, collections of seed or rooted cuttings grown in plastic packs can be placed outdoors on top of rectangular plastic flats, or pans that have drainage holes and are halfway filled with sand. Use flats stacked two or three deep to support the weight of the sand and plants.

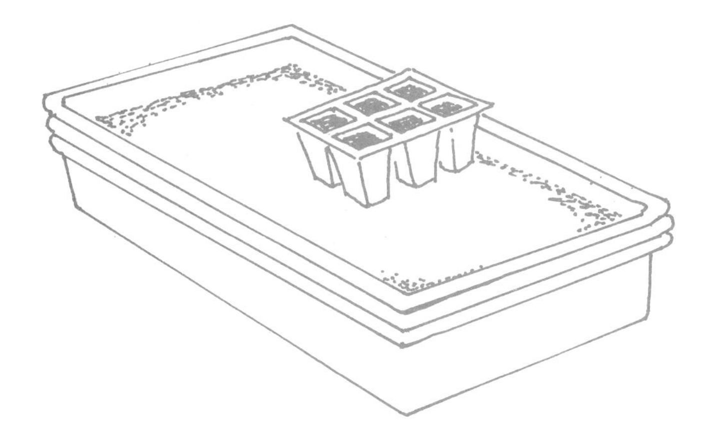

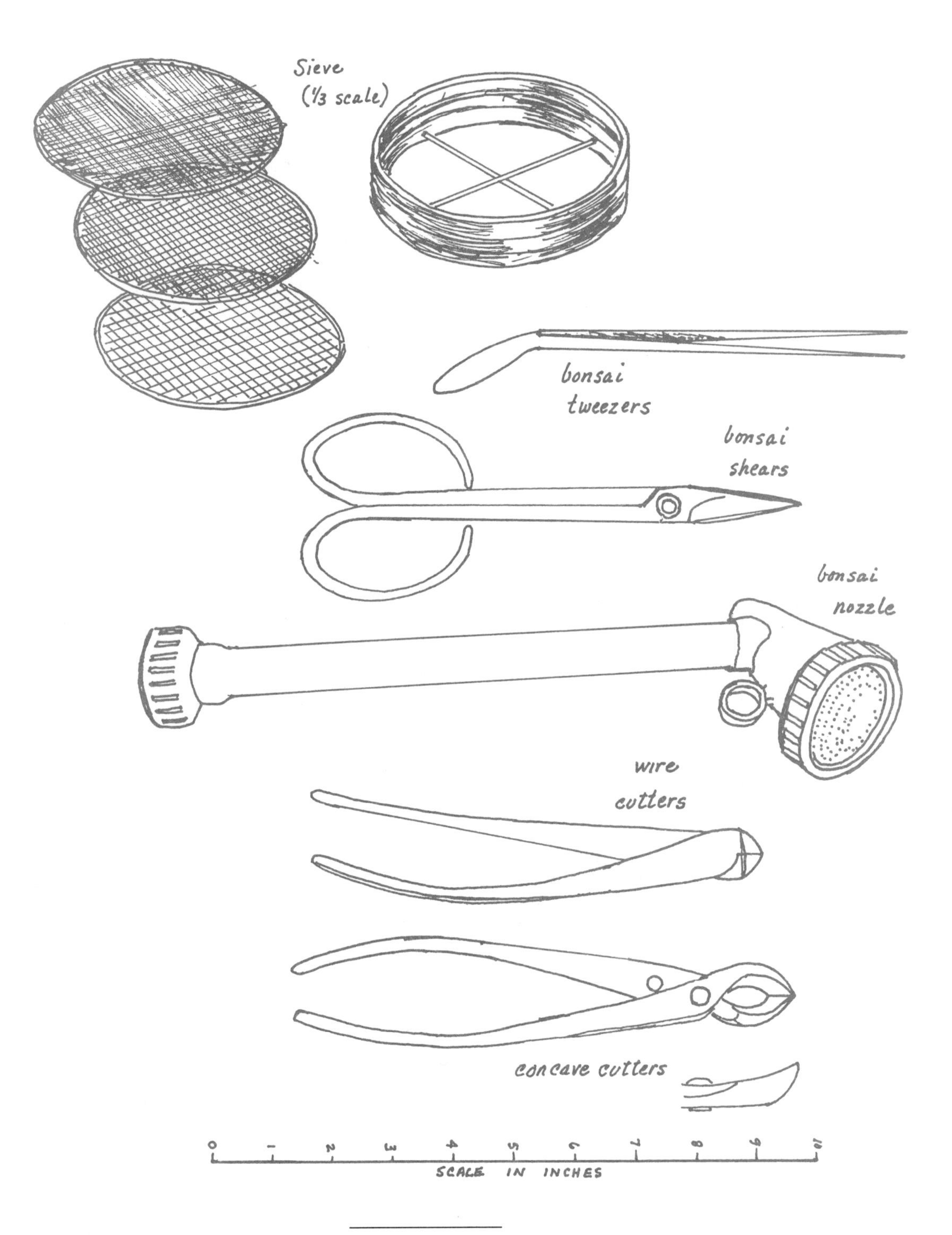
Sieve
(1/3 scale)
bonsai
tweezers
bonsai
shears
bonsai
nozzle
wire
cutters
concave cutters
0
1
2
3
4
5
6
7
8
9
10
SCALE IN INCHES

Tools

KEEP A SUPPLY of good tools handy in pockets, a leather sheath, or a carrying box when working with plants. For small plants a small instrument is necessary. Iris scissors (referring to the iris of the human eye) are perfect for tiny plants. Forceps or large tweezers are best for grooming, and come in different sizes. They are helpful in removing dead leaves from the center of plants without damaging the branchlets or flower buds.

Shops that carry tools for bonsai enthusiasts also carry implements that are useful in training herbs:

bonsai tweezers
bonsai shears
watering nozzle (a fine nozzle to fit the end of a hose)
concave cutters (to remove stubs and allow cambium to grow over scars)
sieves (a set of three from one-quarter inch down in size)
wire cutters (specially made to remove bonsai wires)
scoops (stainless steel with a screening insert to remove dustlike particles from soil, which will clog up air spaces)

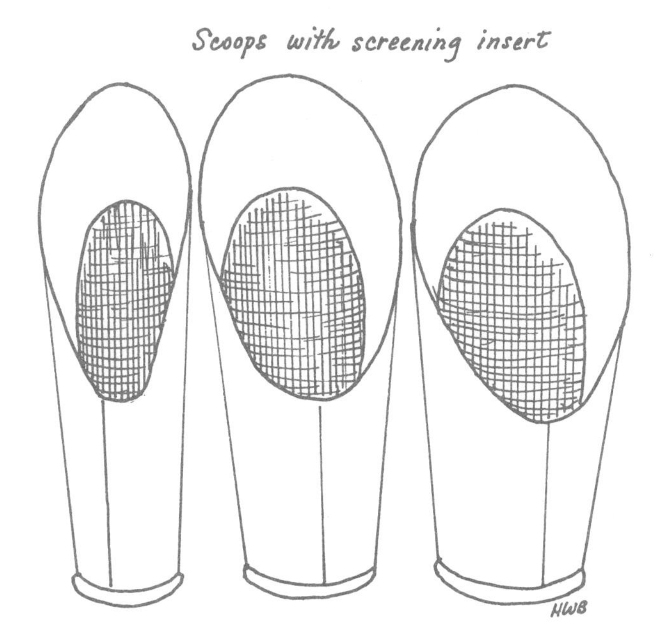

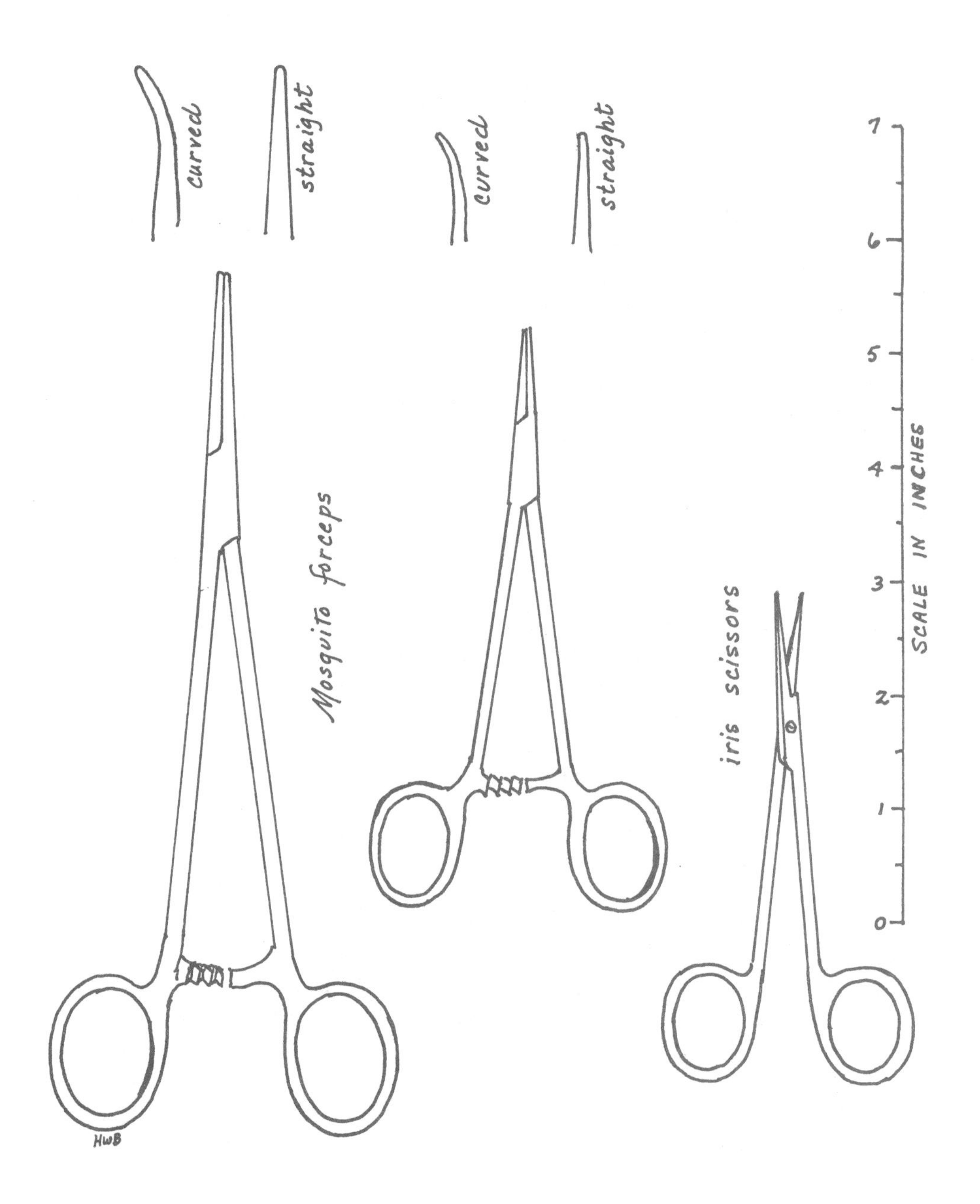
curved
straight
curved
straight
Mosquito forceps
iris scissors
SCALE IN INCHES
0
1
2
3
4
5
6
7
HWB

All of the above are available at Midwest Bonsai Pottery or other shops that carry bonsai supplies. The following tools can be ordered from Brookstone Hard-to-Find Tools:

curved mosquito forceps	5″	#01587
	5½″	#01253
straight mosquito forceps	5″	#01586
	5½″	#01252
iris scissors		#01667

Winter Care

MOST OF our cooking herbs come from the Mediterranean, where winter temperatures remain above freezing throughout the entire year. An ideal spot for indoor growing is a cool greenhouse or glass house, which maintains daytime temperatures of 50°F and 40°F at night. Woody herbs, such as santolina, sweet bay, and rosemary, need a cool winter. Indoors a sunny window is best; the temperature should not exceed 60°F.

A winter plant room with white walls, a white ceiling, and a brightly colored floor is an ideal growing environment, as plants respond to lots of light. If the humidity indoors is less than 40 percent, place the herbs on trays of wet pebbles or use a humidifier.

If tender herbs are brought indoors during the winter months it is advisable to cut them back severely, keep them cool, and water them only about once a week at the most. Of course, severe cutback is not possible with trained plants when the object is to encourage growth. To reduce the shock of severe temperature changes, try bringing plants indoors when the night temperatures outside are still the same as those inside.

Plants can go back outdoors in the spring when the night temperatures are about the same as they have experienced indoors all winter. Plants must be exposed to the sun gradually. Start them on the north side of the house, gradually allowing them one half hour more of sun each day.

Cleaning Pots

ALWAYS RINSE pots with cold water, using a nylon Tuffy or pot and pan scrubber. Then soak them in a plastic tub containing one part bleach and five parts water. This will remove algae, fungi, and lichens. After a few hours in the bleach solution, rinse the pots well in cold water and allow them to dry.

To remove white salts that accumulate on pots in areas of the country where the water is alkaline, give pots a vinegar bath. Vinegar is available in gallon jugs at food markets. Do not dilute the vinegar as it is only 5 percent acetic acid. After a day's soak the salts should loosen up, but again transfer the pots to the cold water tap and scrub all areas, while they are wet, with a nylon Tuffy. Let them dry completely. If white salts reappear, repeat the vinegar bath. If repeated baths are necessary, make sure to use a fresh vinegar solution as the salts will eventually neutralize the cleansing properties of the vinegar.

If there is space outdoors, clay pots may be stored exposed to the elements. After several months of exposure to the rain they will be cleansed of their alkaline deposits and look like new.

In some areas of the country soap and water scrubbing will suffice. But do not store the pots in stacks until they are completely dry. It is only when clay pots are completely dry that salts show up.

I do not advise putting clay pots in the dishwasher. At the last of many visits from dishwasher repair persons I was told that they'd never seen such a late model dishwasher in such terrible shape!

Top Dressing

TOP DRESSING not only makes a pleasing setting for a plant but also gives uniformity to a container-grown collection. Top dressing holds moisture in the soil and discourages the growth of weeds. If perlite has been used in the soil mixture, top dressing will conceal the white particles that work their way to the surface and detract from the plant's appearance. However, if you water with too harsh a spray, the top dressing will be invaded by perlite and charcoal rising from out of the soil.

There are several top dressings from which to choose:

Charcoal: Lightweight and very black. It will float if the plant is watered with too much force.

Terra-Green (or Turface): Earth-colored and lightweight, it comes in three sizes. It is a montmorillonite mineral (containing fine clay particles), is sterile, has a neutral pH, and is inert. Remarkably porous.

Grit (traction grit or poultry grit): Grey limestone in the Midwest, beige granite in the East.

Bark: Heavier, bulkier. Best for large containers. A fine color. Small pine bark chips are attractive. In the long run, however, bark chips will compete with the plant for nitrogen.

Cinders: A deep reddish brown.

Pebbles: Grey limestone in the Midwest, beige granite in the East.

A general rule for top dressing: the smaller the plant the finer the top dressing should be.

Cleaning Pebbles

Place a small amount of pebbles in a sieve. Place the sieve in a container, balanced on the rim, and run cold water over the pebbles, stirring to dislodge debris that floats. Place the cleaned pebbles in a clean container and repeat the process with another small amount of soiled pebbles.

The Local Garden Center

A WORD ABOUT local garden centers. While they do not have room for every horticultural product or every fine plant, customers should encourage their local garden centers to provide new products and plants that merit attention. Often garden center managers are unaware of new developments, or have not had the time to do research or go to conferences. Customers can do both the garden center and the buying public a favor by providing information on better products.

Traffic

KEEP ALL POTTED, precious plants away from traffic—that is, children, workers, bicycles, toys, and delivery people. Here are two personal tales of woe.

One day as a carpenter prepared to mount a ladder in order to clean out a rain gutter, I questioned him as to the safety of my rosemary standard nearby. "Oh no," he said, "that plant isn't in my way." But instead of working from the ladder, he chose to go up onto the slippery shake roof. He promptly fell into my rosemary, knocking out one-sixth of its head. He had my deep sympathy, but I think his broken leg healed much faster than my rosemary!

Another time, friends came to visit—on bicycles. My thoughts at the moment were on other things, and I didn't pay attention to where they parked their bikes. This being the Windy City, the wind soon blew over a bicycle which fell onto two bonsai. The forest planting of *Carpinus japonica* lost only minor branches, but the *Juniperus procumbens* 'Nana' had its trunk snapped. The bonsai doctor had to drill a hole through the injury and secure it with a thin screw and bolt. I only hope that the cambium will grow over this hardware.

Grey-leaf Herbs

Silver-, grey-, and white-leaf plants are extremely difficult to grow in hot, humid climates. They do best with days of warm sunshine and low humidity and hot, dry winds. If left in the rain, high heat, and humidity, their centers will rot.

The silver is formed by a coating of hairs or fuzz that helps the plants survive during the hot, dry weather of their native habitat. The hairs deflect the rays of the sun and conserve moisture by keeping transpiration from the leaves and stems to a minimum.

Silver plants need to be kept dry and top-dressed with pebbles or grit to keep the stems and leaves dry at soil level and allow for air circulation. Never top-dress grey plants with organic mulch.

The following grey-leaf herbs are very difficult to grow in heat and humidity, but are worth trying:

Achillea tomentosa—woolly yarrow
Antennaria dioica—catsfoot, pussy-toes
Chrysanthemum haradjanii (from Syria)
Euryops evansii
Euryops pectinatus (a South African daisy)
Helichrysum italicum ssp. *siitalicum* 'Nana'*—dwarf curry plant
Helichrysum petiolatum—licorice plant
Helichrysum psilolepsis
Marrubium vulgare—horehound
Santolina chamaecyparissus—grey lavender cotton
Santolina chamaecyparissus 'Nana'—dwarf silver lavender cotton

Remember that certain plants creeping over large stones in hot climates will probably have their stems and leaves cooked. While some grey plants and creeping thymes can withstand this situation, they are still extremely difficult to grow in hot, humid, rainy weather. If grown vertically (as in strawberry jar pockets) these problems can be avoided.

If silver-leaf plants are moved into the shade, the leaves will turn green. They will revert if moved back into the sun.

*Old name: *H. angustifolium* 'Nana'

In Summary

TO GROW award-winning plants one must have the will to succeed, plenty of energy, and time set aside each day for tending the plants. Nurturing plants demands knowledge of horticulture, dedication, and keen powers of observation. Whether in competition or for one's own pleasure, a well-grown plant is a most rewarding achievement.

CHAPTER 2

An Herbal Strawberry Jar

OR THOSE with limited outdoor space, a strawberry jar is an alternative container for growing herbs that can also serve as a decorative focal point. By using culinary herbs, one has the added option of using the herbs for cooking.

Readily available from most garden centers, strawberry jars come in different sizes with varying numbers of pockets. The larger the jar the more herbs can be grown and the more space will be available for the herbs' large root systems.

A jar with more than six side pockets should have a polyvinyl chloride (PVC) tube in the center in order to distribute water to each pocket. Cut the tube about four inches shorter than the outside height measurement of the jar, and drill holes in the tube at the exact levels of the pockets (see box).

I use a well-drained soil consisting of one part compost or commercial potting soil; one part Canadian sphagnum peat moss put through a one-quarter-inch sieve and moistened with hot water; and two parts perlite, which is light (a suitable substitute called Torpedo Sand [grade #FA2] is heavier). One can also use a soilless mix.

HWB

Planting

WHEN DECIDING which plant to put into which pocket, think in terms of color, texture, growth habit, and eventual plant size.

Assemble the plants—that have been grown in two- to four-inch pots.

Place a small piece of screening over the jar's drainage hole. Then place the PVC tube in the center of the jar and add soil up to the bottom tier of holes.

Remove each plant from its container and dip its roots into a bucket of water, washing off enough soil so that the roots may be inserted into a pocket opening. Cover the roots, making certain that the plant is firmly established in the soil. The plant should have its former soil level on an even plane with the lip of the pocket, allowing for plant sinkage which might occur after a good rain.

After planting the first tier of pockets, add more soil and continue planting the second and third tiers in the same manner until the soil is about four inches from the top of the jar. To avoid spilling soil onto the lower plants, cover them with a small rag, tissue, or aluminum foil.

For the top of the jar, choose a larger plant that will grow in scale and proportion to the central opening. Place this plant over the PVC tube, center it, and carefully add soil all around its root system, tamping the soil—not the root ball—with a chopstick or the eraser end of a long pencil. Top-dress this large opening with fine gravel or commercially available Terra-Green (Turface). Top dressing makes a neat finish, keeps the perlite from rising to the top, preserves moisture, and keeps plant foliage from being splashed with soil during watering.

Caring for the Plants

WATER THE JAR initially by soaking the bottom in a large pan of water for a couple of hours. The water level should be no higher than the bottom of the lowest pocket. Then, using a fine rose on a watering can, water slowly and carefully all around the rim of the top of the jar.

Keep the jar in full sun (at least five hours a day) and rotate it clockwise at least twice a week so that all plants receive equal light exposure. Fertilize with 20-20-20 once a month. Using the manufacturer's formula given on the label, these diluted soluble salts can be applied with a watering can.

Identification of plants in Strawberry Jar

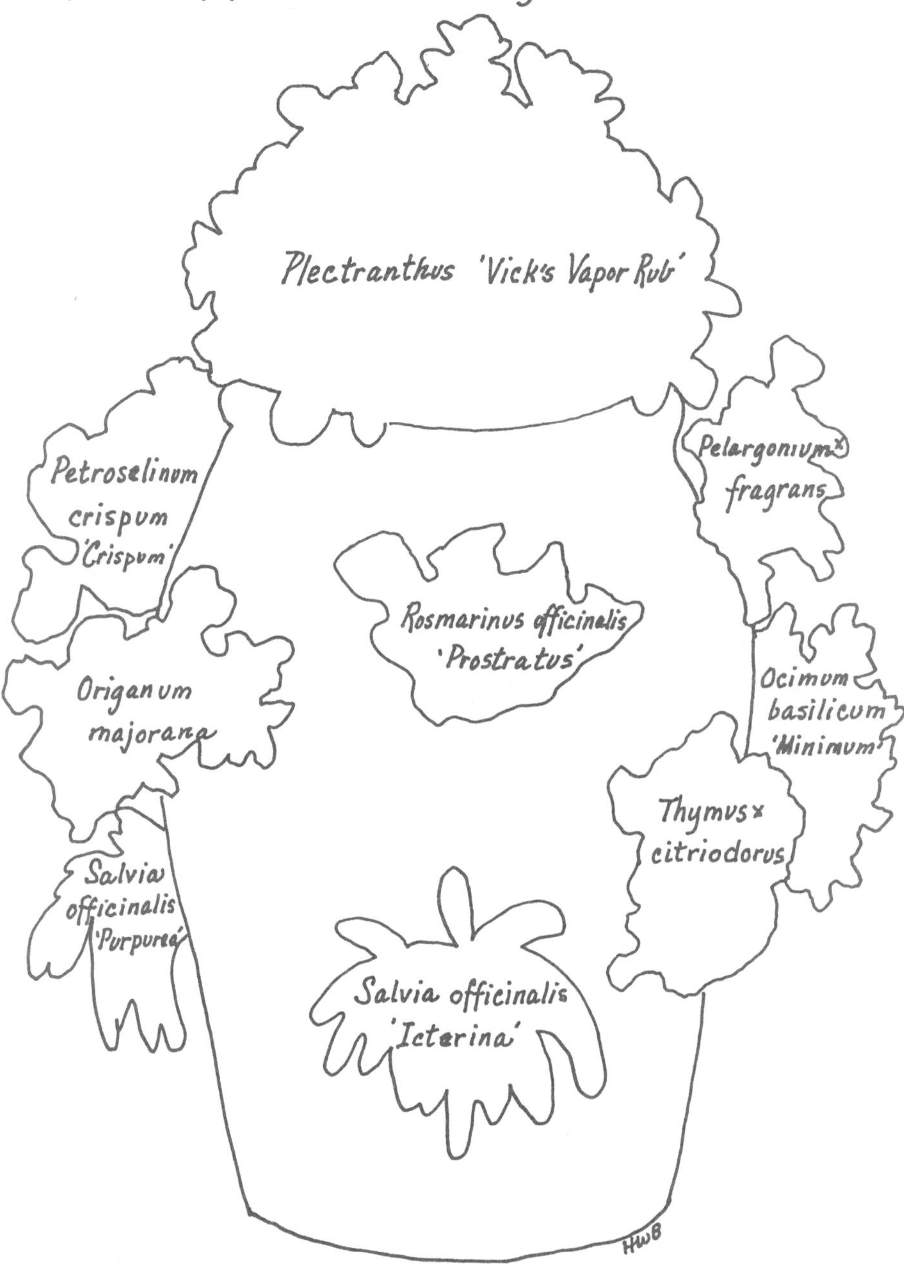

In order to grow compact plants that remain in scale, pinch the plants back frequently. Do not let annual herbs like basil set flower buds—cut them off. When herbs bloom and set seed they stop producing oils.

My personal preference is that the plants should not touch. I like to see each plant framed by the earth color of the clay jar.

Leave the herbal strawberry jar out even in rainy weather. If a well-drained soil mixture is used there is little danger of root rot occurring during prolonged periods of moisture.

During periods of drought, herbs should be watered diligently whenever the soil has dried out. With temperatures over 90°F and strong breezes, daily watering will be necessary. The Mediterranean plants enjoy being dry, but parsley from the Umbelliferae (carrot family) and savory from the Labiatae (mint family) need more water, particularly after these plants have produced large root systems.

Herbs can survive a winter indoors but will not look as well as when they are outside in the sun. House temperatures tend to be too warm for the plants and often there is insufficient light. After the first frost, dismantle the jar and consign the plants to the compost pile. If the grower has both the patience and the space, cuttings could be made from the perennial herbs prior to the first frost (see Chapter 9: Propagation of Some Ornamental Herbs). If, however, a cool greenhouse is available with extra space, the jar can be wintered there. Be on the alert for insects such as aphids that tend to appear on the parsley.

Much pleasure can be derived in cultivating a strawberry jar of herbs. The plants and container take up little room, are delightful to look at, and harvesting the herbs for cooking is a deliciously rewarding bonus.

Suggested Herbs for Strawberry Jars

Top

Lavandula dentata—French lavender
Lavandula stoechas—French lavender, Spanish lavender
Pelargonium graveolens 'Lady Plymouth'—Lady Plymouth geranium
Petroselinum crispum 'Crispum'—curly parsley
Plectranthus amboinicus—Cuban oregano, Spanish thyme, Indian borage
Plectranthus 'Vick's Vapor Rub'—menthol plant, Vick's plant
Salvia officinalis 'Nana'—dwarf garden sage
Tropaeolum nanum 'Tom Thumb'—dwarf compact nasturtium

Pockets

Allium schoenoprasum—chives (very upright)
Helichrysum italicum ssp. *siitalicum* 'Nana'—dwarf curry plant
Mentha pulegium—pennyroyal (keep well watered)
Mentha requienii—Corsican mint (keep well watered; needs more shade with temperatures greater than 90°F)
Ocimum basilicum 'Minimum'—bush basil
Ocimum basilicum 'Spicy Globe'—spicy globe basil
Origanum dictamnus—Dittany of Crete (grey)
Origanum majorana—sweet marjoram
Origanum vulgare ssp. *vulgare* 'Aureum'—golden oregano
Origanum vulgare ssp. *hirtum*—Greek oregano, best Italian
Pelargonium abrotanifolium—southernwood geranium
Pelargonium 'Little Gem'—little gem geranium (rose scented)
Pelargonium 'Prince Rupert Variegated'—Prince Rupert variegated geranium
Pelargonium x fragens—nutmeg geranium
Pelargonium nervosum—lime geranium
Perargonium odoratissimum—apple geranium
Petroselinum crispum 'Crispum'—curly parsley
Rosmarinus officinalis 'Prostratus'—prostrate rosemary
Salvia officinalis 'Icterina'—golden sage
Salvia officinalis 'Purpuracens'—purple sage
Salvia officinalis 'Tricolor'—tricolor sage

Santolina chamaecyparissus 'Nana'—dwarf silver lavender cotton
Satureja thymbra—thymbra savory
Teucrium aroanium
Teucrium majoricum
Teucrium marum—cat thyme
Thymus 'Argenteus'—silver thyme (upright)
Thymus 'Broad-leaf English'—English thyme (upright)
Thymus caespititius (T. azoricus)—tiny thyme, tufted thyme
Thymus x citriodorus—lemon thyme
Thymus herba-barona—caraway thyme (procumbent)
Thymus praecox ssp. *arcticus* cultivars—creeping thyme (use any of these cultivars)
Thymus vulgaris 'Narrow-leaf French'—French thyme (erect to open-spreading)

Too large for strawberry jars

Anethum graveolens—dill
Artemisia dracunculus 'Sativa'—French tarragon
Mints (except Corsican and pennyroyal)
Ocimum basilicum—sweet basil (the leaves are awfully large)
Petroselinum crispum 'Neopolitanum'—Italian parsley
Tropaeolum majus—nasturtium

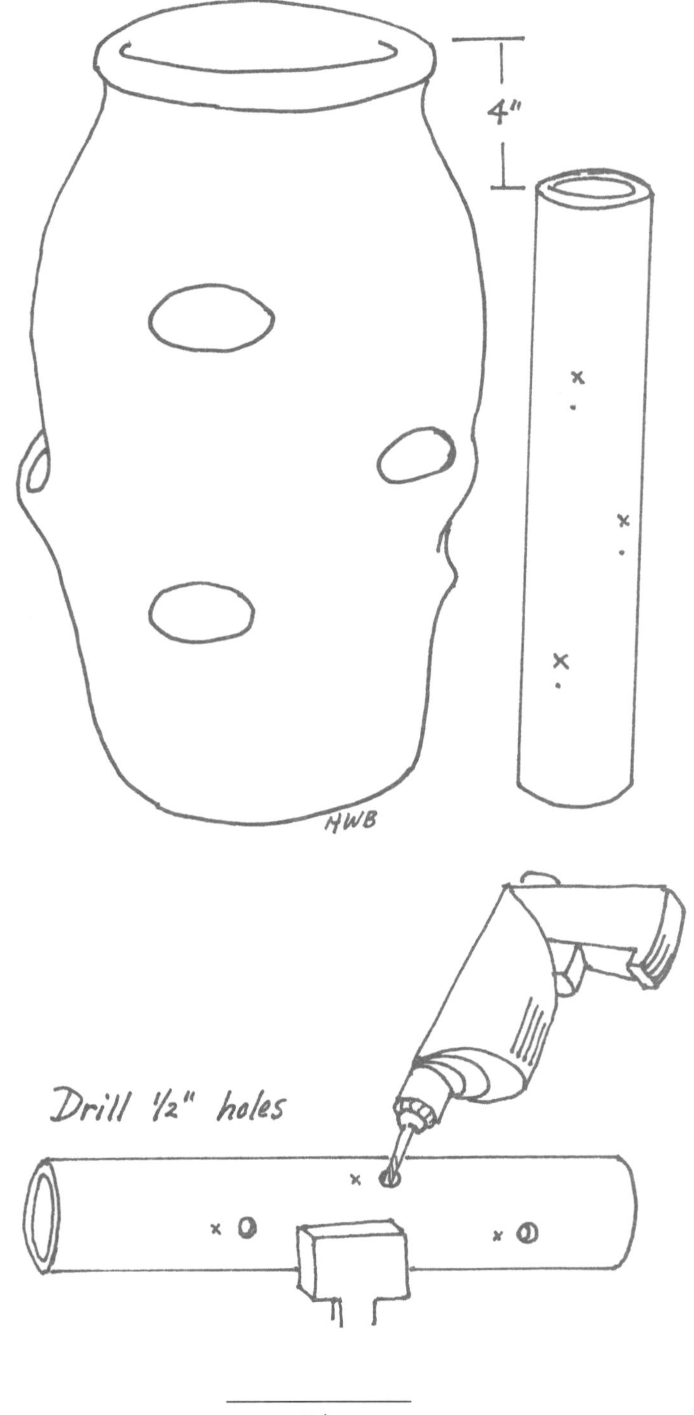
4"
HWB
Drill ½" holes

Making a Plastic Watering Tube

PLASTIC (PVC) TUBING comes in many sizes. Use a two-, three-, or four-inch diameter tube, depending on the size of your strawberry jar. Cut it four inches shorter than the total outside height of the jar. Using an electric drill, make holes in the tubing to correspond with the location of the root balls of the inserted plants. Start by marking, with a waterproof pen, the places where the holes should be—after allowing for an inch of elevation at the bottom end, as the tube must sit inside the jar on top of its drainage hole. Check the markings to make sure they are at the right level and then drill holes, at least one-half inch in diameter.

Place plastic mesh screening on the bottom of the tube, wiring it in circular fashion around the end. Fill the tube with pebbles, which will diffuse the water, sending some of it through the side holes. Tamp several times to secure the pebbles. Cover the top of the tube with plastic screening and wire it in place.

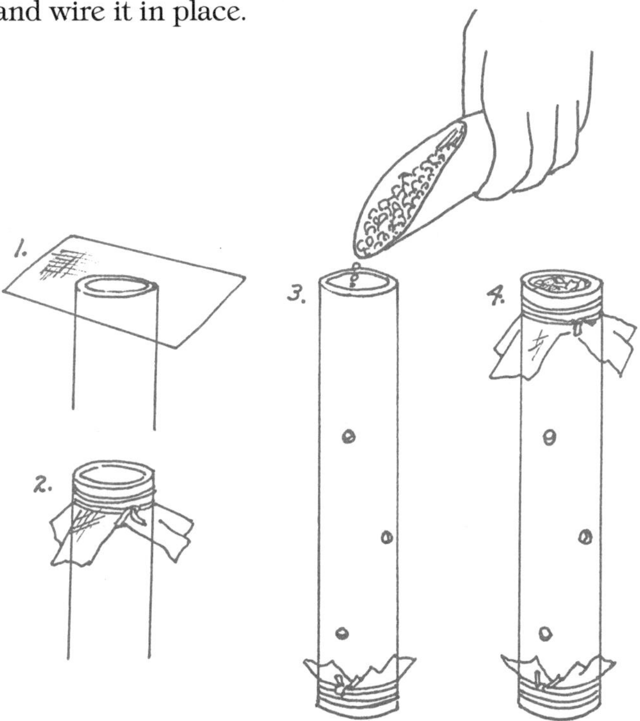

A Plan for Planting

1. Assemble the plants, one for each pocket.

2. Assemble a flat pan (a large cookie sheet will do), a PVC tube, a piece of plastic screening approximately 3″ × 3″, a scoop, a chopstick, sharp scissors, top dressing, the strawberry jar, a bucket of water, a container of pebbles, and a container of mixed soil.

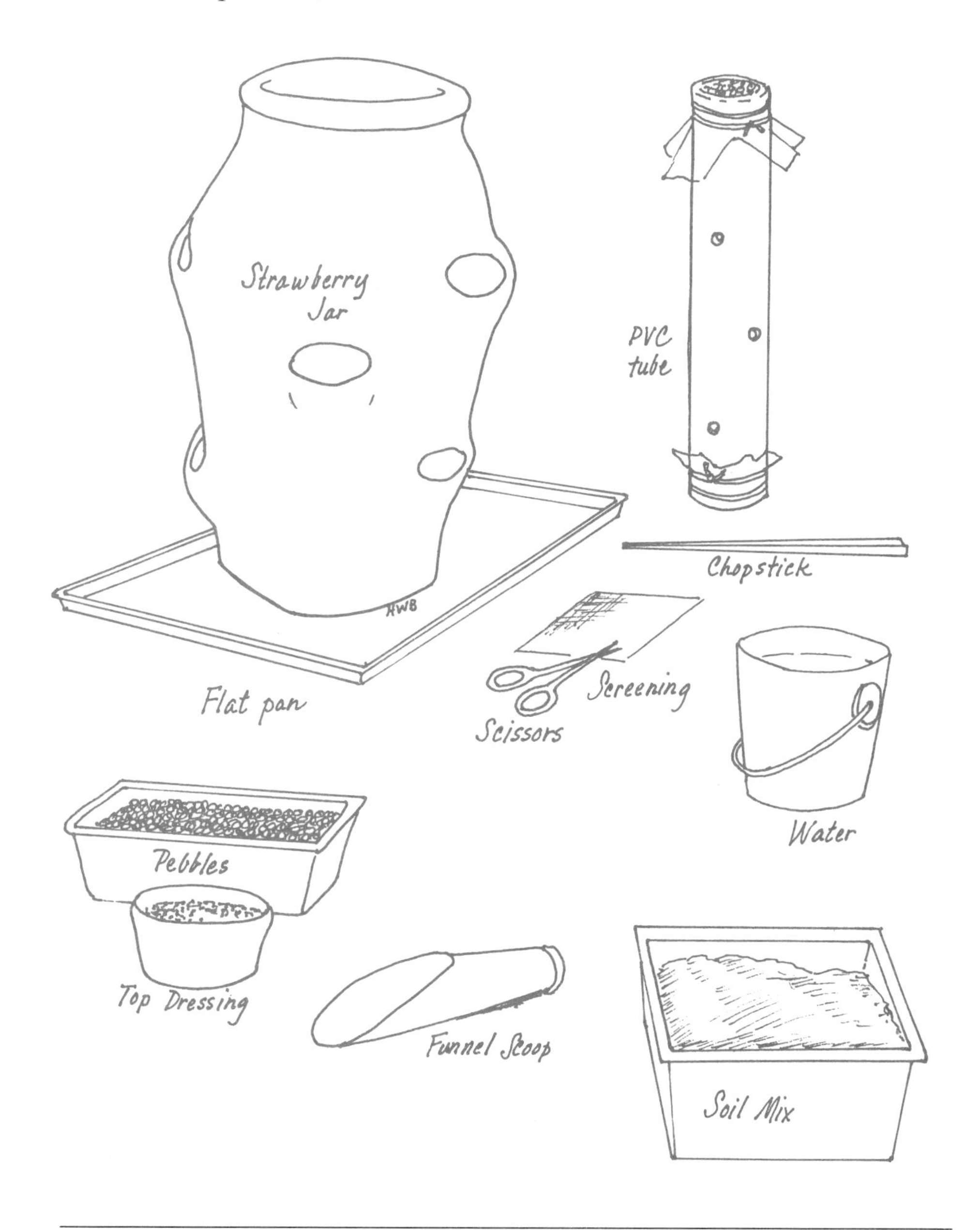

3. Place the jar on the flat pan. Place the plastic mesh screening over the drainage hole. Insert the PVC tube so that it rests on top of the drainage hole. Using the scoop, fill the jar with soil up to the level of the bottom tier of pockets.

4. Decide which plant is to go where.

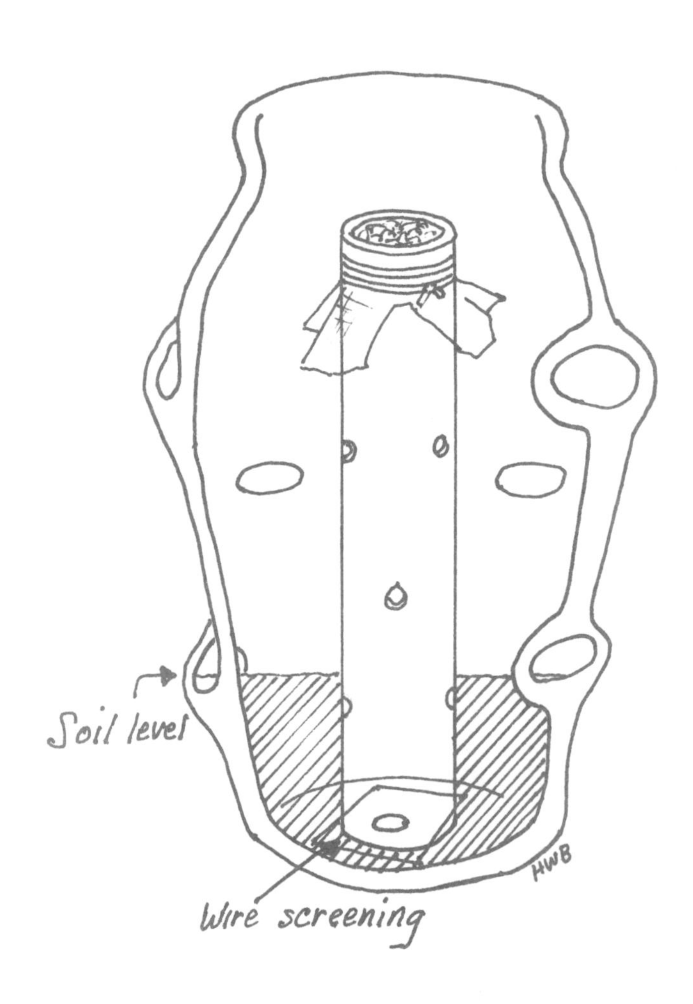

5. Remove the plants from their containers. Dip the root balls in water, reducing their size until they are slightly smaller than the pocket openings. (It may be necessary to cut away some long roots.) Put the plant's label loosely into the center of each plant.

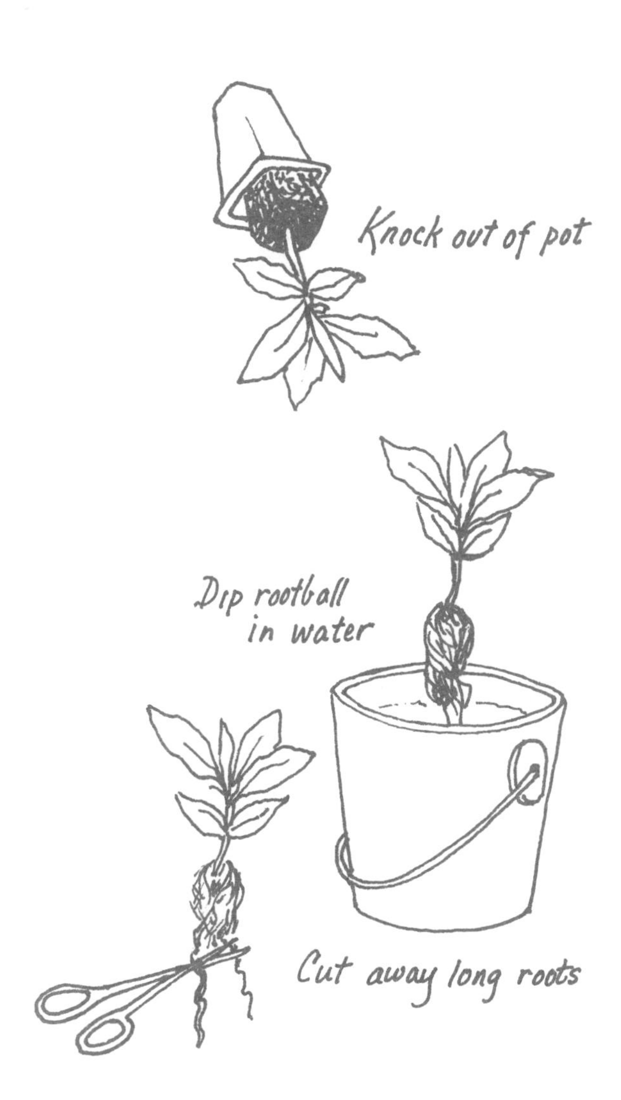

6. With the chopstick, gently push the ball into the pocket, pointing the roots downward and keeping the crown, or old soil level on the plant, level with the pocket lip. (The plants invariably sink.)

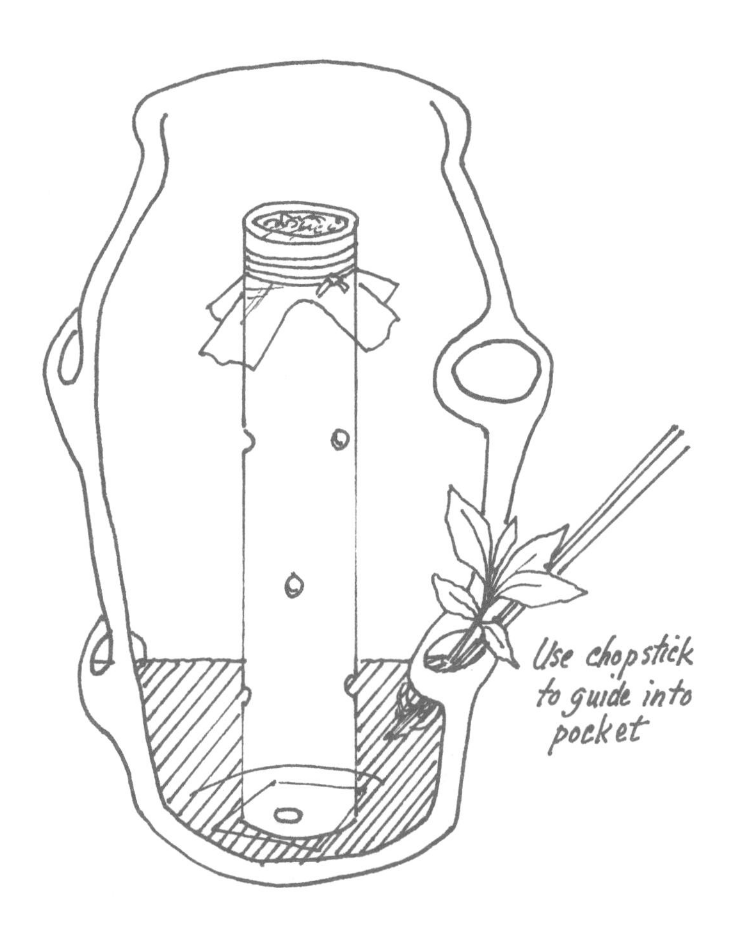

7. Reaching down from the top, cover the roots well with your fingers as you push the soil up around the root ball. Tamp the soil from the outside with your chopstick, around the roots, but do not tamp the root ball.

8. Repeat this process for each pocket, tier by tier.

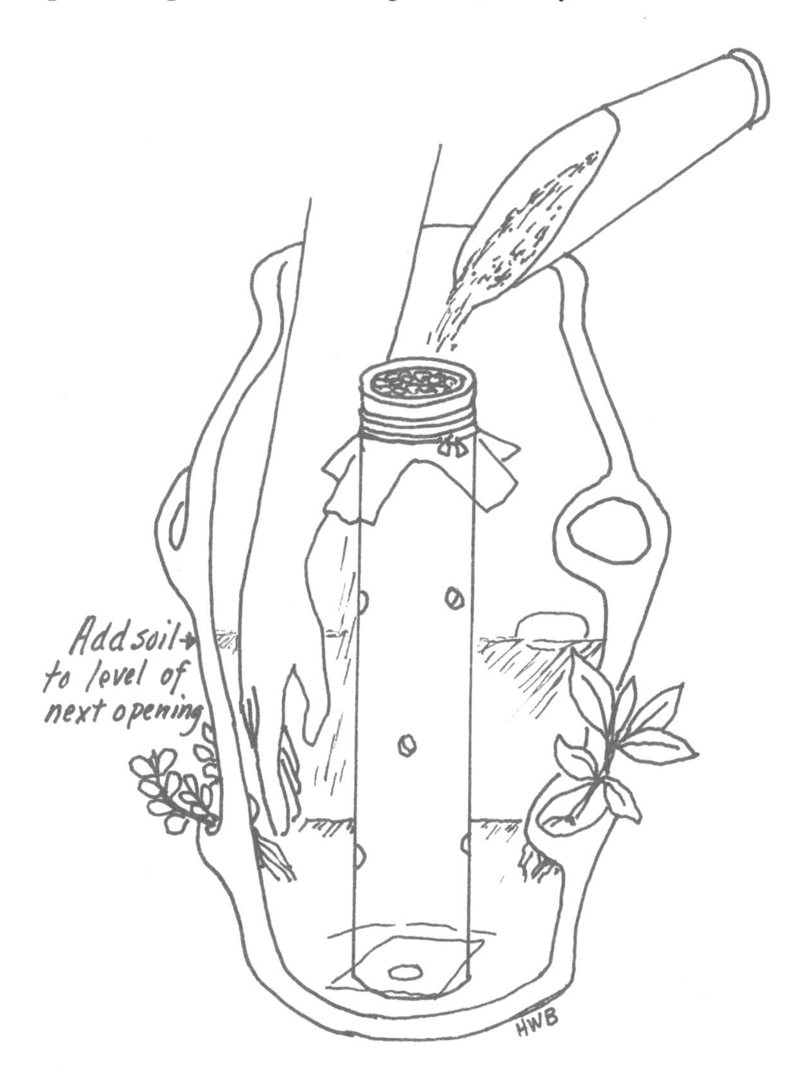

9. When all the pockets are planted and there remains about a four-inch space at the top, insert the larger plant, place its root ball in the center over the PVC tube and fill in all around it, first with soil and then with one-half inch of top dressing. Depending on the size of the jar, this layer should be three-quarters of an inch to one inch below the rim of the jar. The top dressing should be Terra-Green, but grit could also be used.

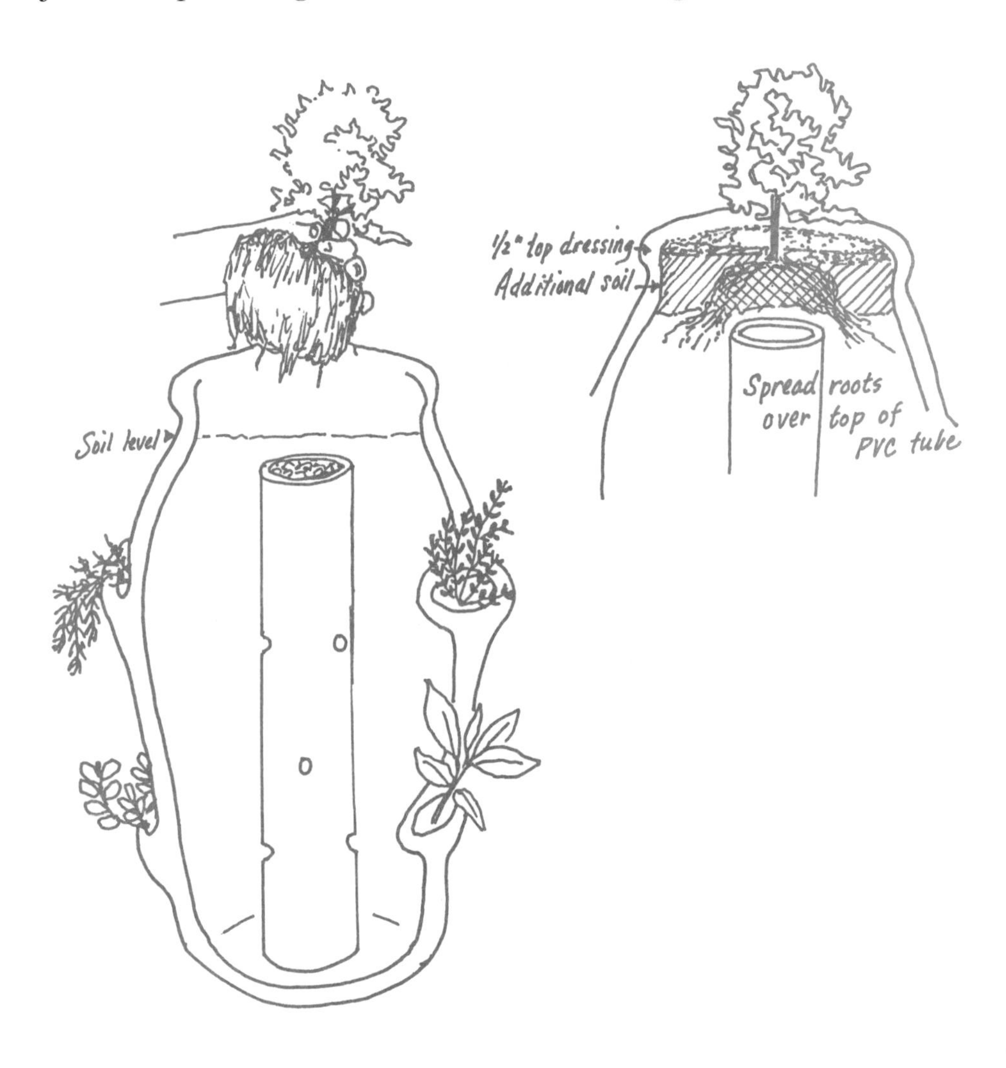

10. Make a diagram of the jar on paper, with a waterproof pen, identifying each plant. Remove the labels from each plant and keep them with the diagram for reference.

11. Water the jar by soaking the bottom in a pan of water filled no higher than the bottom of the lowest pocket. Then, using a fine rose on a watering can, water all around the top.

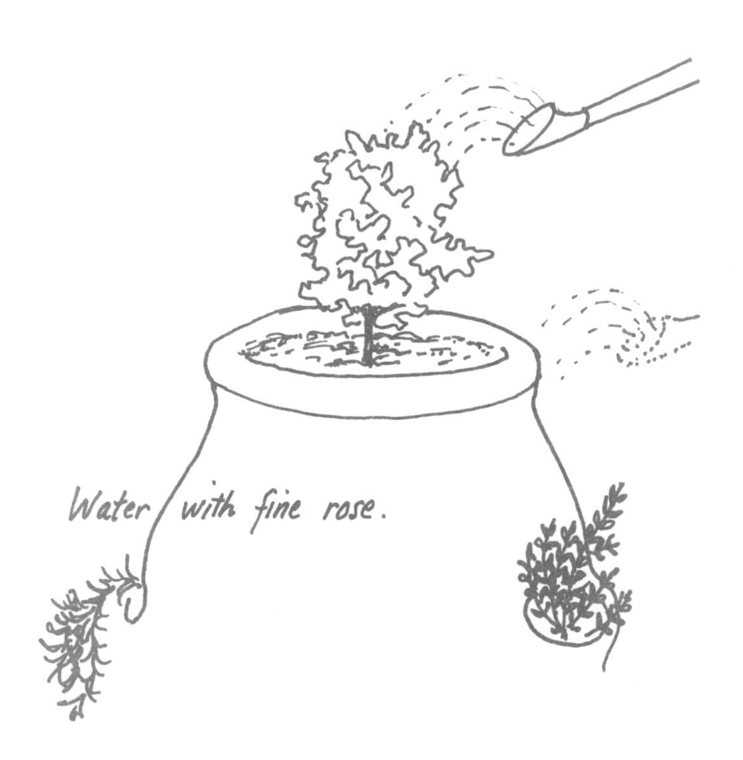

Ocimum basilicum

Thymus x citriodorus

Salvia officinalis 'Icterina'

Petroselinum crispum 'Crispum'

Rosmarinus officinalis 'Prostratus'

CHAPTER 3

A Window Box of Herbs

FOR GARDENERS with limited growing space or limited time for gardening, a window box of herbs, particularly the culinary ones, is ideal. The box can be kept outside a window, on a balcony, on a deck, on a doorstep, or on a driveway. The only placement requirement is that the window box should be located in a spot that receives at least five hours of sun daily.

Choosing and Mounting the Box

WOOD IS THE MOST attractive material for a window box. A ready-made container may be purchased at a garden center, or one can be made. If you elect to make your own window box, use wood one-inch thick; redwood or cedar are good choices, but expensive. White pine can be used, but it must be treated to protect it against the weather. Wood preservatives containing pentachlorophenol, or creosote, should not be used as they are toxic to plants; copper naphthenate and copper sulfate are safer, when used as the manufacturer directs.

Metal boxes are undesirable, as they overheat. Plastic boxes are tougher, lighter, and cheaper but not as pleasing to the eye. While a plastic box can be inserted into a wooden box, thereby prolonging its life, make sure that the drainage holes in both boxes match.

A good size for a window box is three to four feet in length, eight to ten inches wide, and eight to ten inches deep.* The top can slant outwards, making it wider by two inches than the base. Use brass or galvanized screws to hold the wood together, as the weight of moist soil can push nailed boxes apart. Nail one-inch strips of wood to the bottom to allow for drainage if the box is to sit on the ground, a concrete patio, or windowsill.

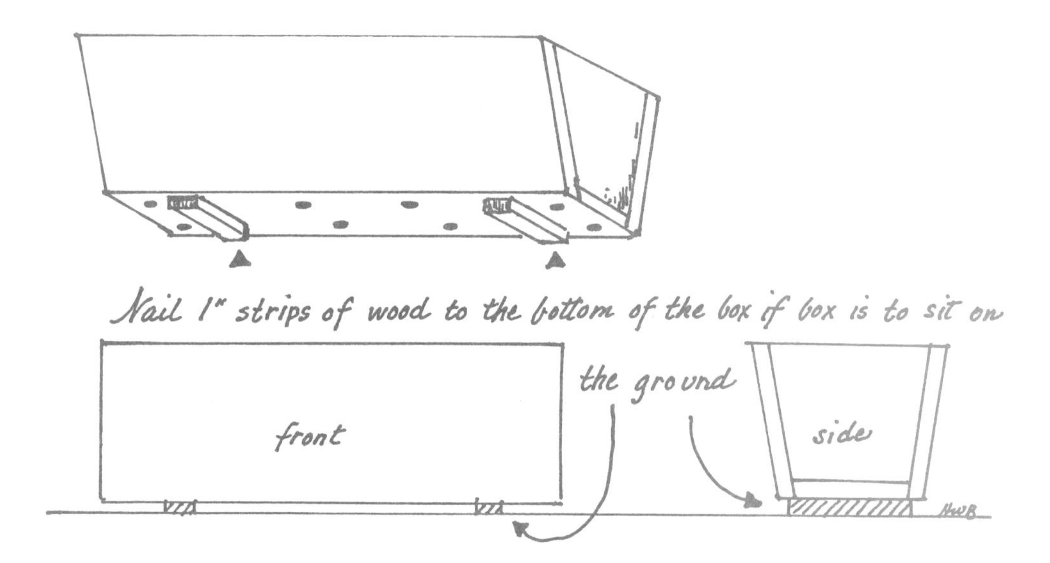

*In planning the size of your box, it may be useful to know that 1″ × 6″ boards are actually ¾″ × 5½″, 1″ × 8″ are ¾″ × 7¼″, and 1″ × 10 are ¾″ × 9½″.

If the sill slants, use wedges underneath the box to make it level.

The window box should contain drainage holes one-half inch in diameter, about eight inches apart. If the box is to be hung outside a window, consider where to drill these holes in relation to where the water from the box will drip.

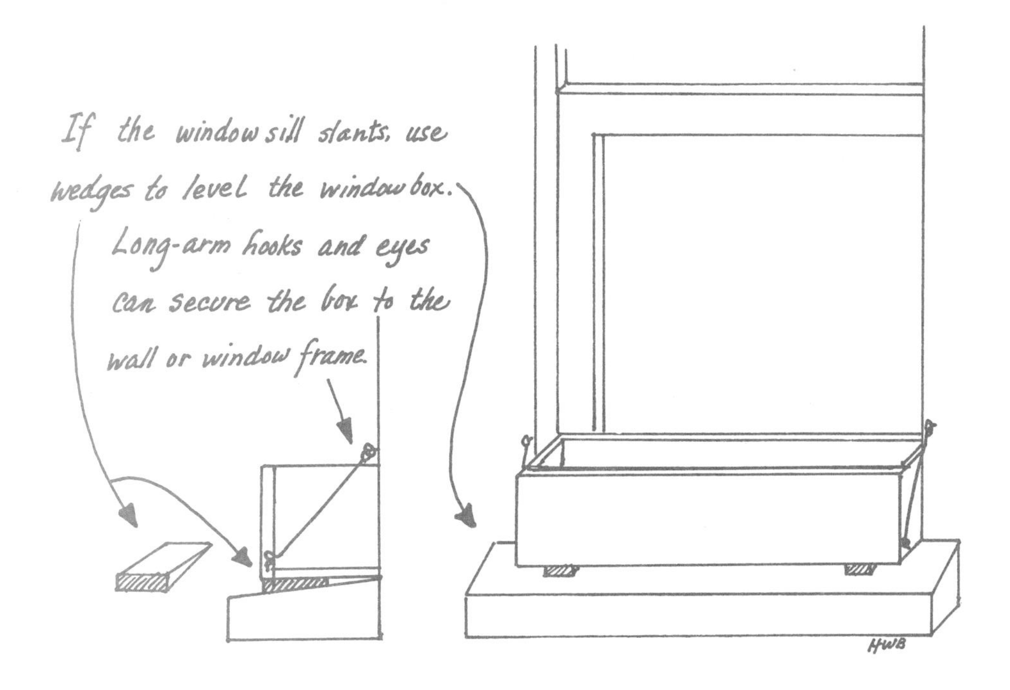

If the box is to be mounted where it could fall and possibly injure someone, it is wise to consult an experienced carpenter, and city building codes should be checked. Plant a mounted box *after* it is in place. If it is to be hung on a balcony railing, mount it securely *inside* the balcony rather than outside, for safety's sake.

A lightweight soil is preferable in window boxes; Grace Metromix #360 is good. The assembled herbs should be in three- or four-inch pots—purchased from a garden center, an herb fair, or ordered by mail from an herb specialty farm.

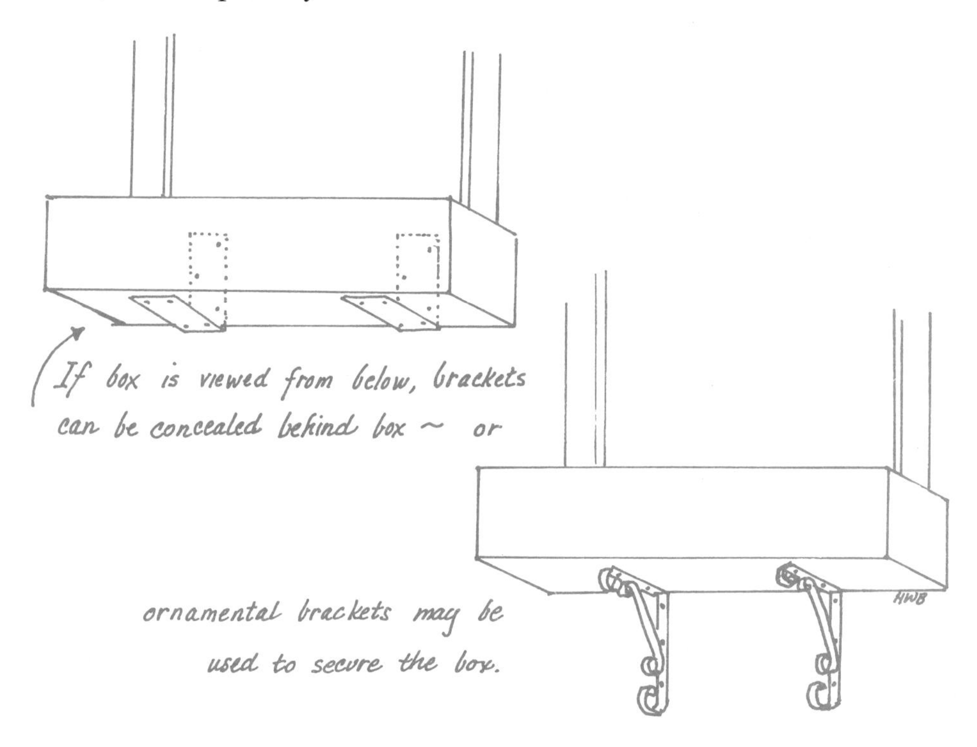

Choosing the Herbs

THE CHOSEN HERBS will probably be culinary or decorative. Try to plant them in a pleasing design with some cascading over the front side of the window box, some globular ones on the sides, and taller ones balanced in between.

Consider leaf texture and color, uprightness, and the spreading or prostrate habits of the plants so that a harmonious, interesting grouping will be achieved. The mature size of a plant should be considered so that the material in the box will be in scale and will allow for visibility from inside the house.

Caring for the Herbs

MAINTENANCE will include watering, fertilizing, snipping to maintain good scale and proportion, removing flowers from the annual herbs, and cutting away dead leaves. Basil must be kept from flowering by removing flower buds. Once flowers appear, the basil will lose its lower leaves and try to set seed in order to reproduce. Another, younger plant can replace a fully mature one.

If daily watering during hot weather is too much bother or not in keeping with one's travel schedule, polymers can be added to the planting soil (discussed under "Soil" in Chapter 1: The Secrets of Growing).

Judicious pruning should discourage the more vigorous plants from overpowering smaller ones. While it is possible to keep herbs for several days in a damp cloth inside a closed plastic bag in the refrigerator, try to use the herbs when they are fresh. If placed in water for a flower arrangement, be sure to remove leaves from the portion of the stem that is in water.

Fertilize the herbs once a week with Peter's 20-20-20 if the plants are growing well and the weather is warm, following the instructions on the label.

Creating a pleasing planting of culinary and fragrant herbs will be a delight from early summer until the first frost. Before the threat of frost, the box may be dismantled or brought into a cool greenhouse. The annual plants may be discarded on the compost pile and the perennials potted up individually, or cuttings may be taken from them to root over winter. The box itself should be well cleaned and stored in a dry, out-of-the-way spot.

A Plan for Planting a Window Box

Assemble materials:
window box
soil
plastic screening
a scoop
a chopstick
top dressing
new plant labels and a waterproof pen (optional)
a watering can
polymers and a large container (optional)

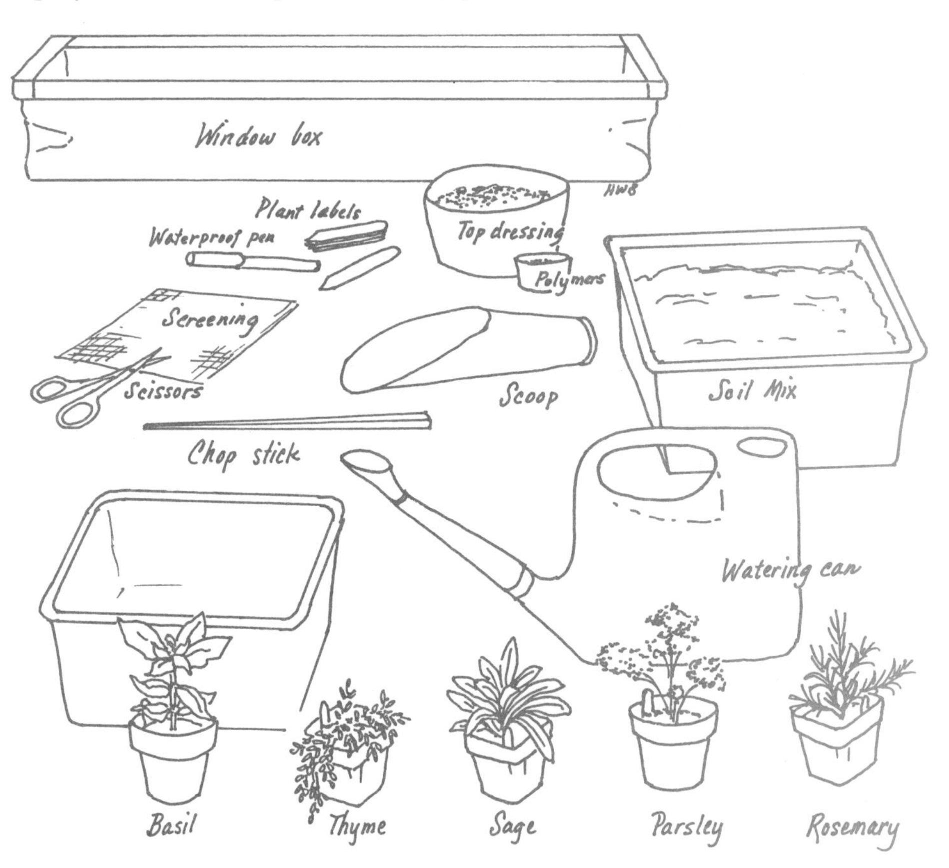

1. Cover the drainage holes of the window box with plastic screening.

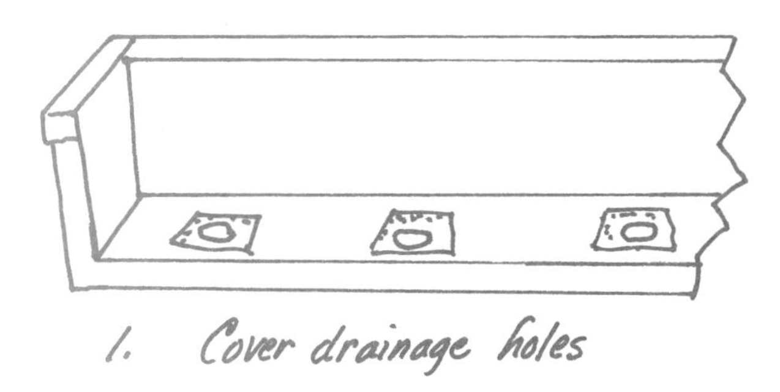

2. Fill the box halfway with soil, having previously mixed the polymers well into the soil in a separate container.

3. Remove the plants from their pots and place them in the window box, remembering to make an attractive design. Keep the plant labels stuck in the center of each root ball. Allow a space five inches in diameter for each plant. Cut the root ball of each plant, slitting the sides and bottom.

4. Add soil, with the scoop, all around the plants. Keep plant foliage clean.
5. Using a chopstick, tamp the soil around each root ball, adding soil as needed.

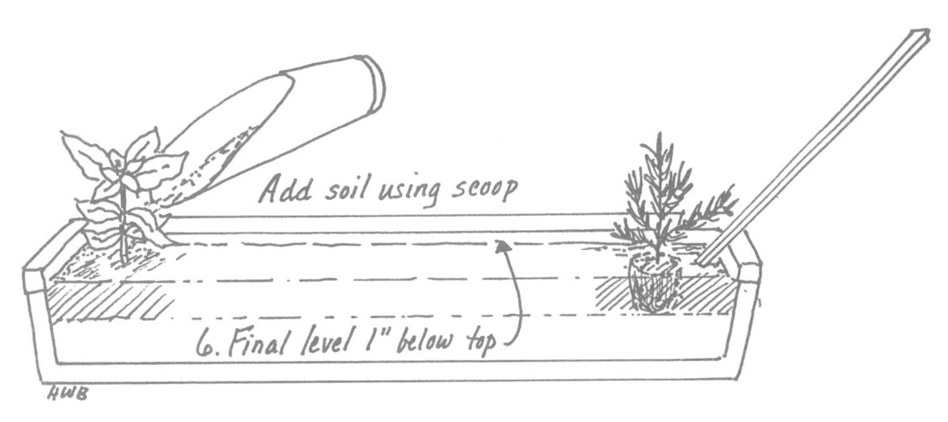

Tamp soil around root ball with chopstick

6. The final soil level should be one inch below the window box rim. The same soil level these plants had in their six-pack should be retained.
7. Remove the plant labels and place them behind each plant, between the side of the box and the soil.
8. Top-dress the entire box, taking care not to get any particles on the leaves.
9. Water, slowly and repeatedly, with a watering can equipped with a fine rose, until all the soil is moist.

Suggested Herbs for Window Boxes

Green Foliage	*Size (in inches)*
Aloysia triphylla—lemon verbena	18–24
Allium schoenoprasum—chives	6–12
Lavandula angustifolia—many cultivars—English lavender	12
Ocimum basilicum 'Minimum'—bush basil	8
Ocimum basilicum 'Spicy Globe'—spicy globe basil	8
Origanum majorana—sweet marjoram	12
Origanum vulgare ssp. *hirtum*—Greek oregano, best Italian	6–12
Petroselinum crispum 'Crispum'—curly parsley	6–12
Rosmarinus officinalis 'Prostratus'—prostrate rosemary	prostrate
Salvia officinalis 'Nana'—dwarf sage	12
Thymus x citriodorus—lemon thyme	6
Thymus praecox ssp. *arcticus*—any creeping thymes	prostrate
Thymus vulgaris—common thyme, cooking thyme	12
Tropaeolum nanum 'Tom Thumb'—dwarf compact nasturtium	6
Purple/Red Foliage	
Ocimum basilicum 'Minimum Purpurascens'—purple bush basil	8
Ocimum basilicum 'Purple Ruffles'—purple ruffles basil	12–24
Ocimum basilicum 'Purpurascens'—dark opal basil	12–24
Salvia officinalis 'Purpurea'—purple sage	12
Yellow/Variegated Foliage	
Myrtus communis 'Microphylla Variegata'—variegated dwarf myrtle	6
Origanum vulgare ssp. *vulgare* 'Areum'—golden marjoram	8

Rosmarinus officinalis 'Joyce DeBaggio'—golden rain rosemary	8
Salvia officinalis 'Icterina'—golden sage	12
Thymus x citriodorus 'Aureus'—golden lemon thyme	6
Thymus 'Clear Gold'—creeping golden thyme	3
Silver Foliage	
Lavandula dentata—French lavender	12–24
Ocimum basilicum 'Silver Fox'—silver fox basil	18
Origanum dictamnus—Dittany of Crete	
Pelargonium x fragrans—nutmeg geranium	6–12
Thymus 'Argenteus'—silver thyme	12
Tricolored Foliage	
Salvia officinalis 'Tricolor'—tricolor sage	12

Pelargonium 'Prince Rupert Variegated'
Plant height:

CHAPTER 4

Creating an Herbal Standard

A STANDARD is a plant with a single straight stem and a head of smaller stems and leaves. It can range from six inches to six feet in height. The size of the head must eventually be trimmed in scale and proportion to the height of the stem—it can be round, triangular, or cone shaped. A pair of identical standards, a real challenge to cultivate, can be a most welcoming sight on either side of the front door of a building, be it an office, apartment, or home. A single standard can be used as an accent in an herb garden, as a focal point in the corner of a garden, or as a decorative addition to a deck, patio, or terrace.

Choosing the Best Herbs

IN GENERAL, the smaller the leaf of the plant, the smaller the standard. The reverse is also true: *Laurus nobilis* (bay laurel) looks well as a five- to six-foot standard. Everyone who cooks is familiar with the three- to four-inch-long leaves, often used in stews and soups. In spring (if greenhouse grown) or summer (if left outside all year), masses of fluffy yellow

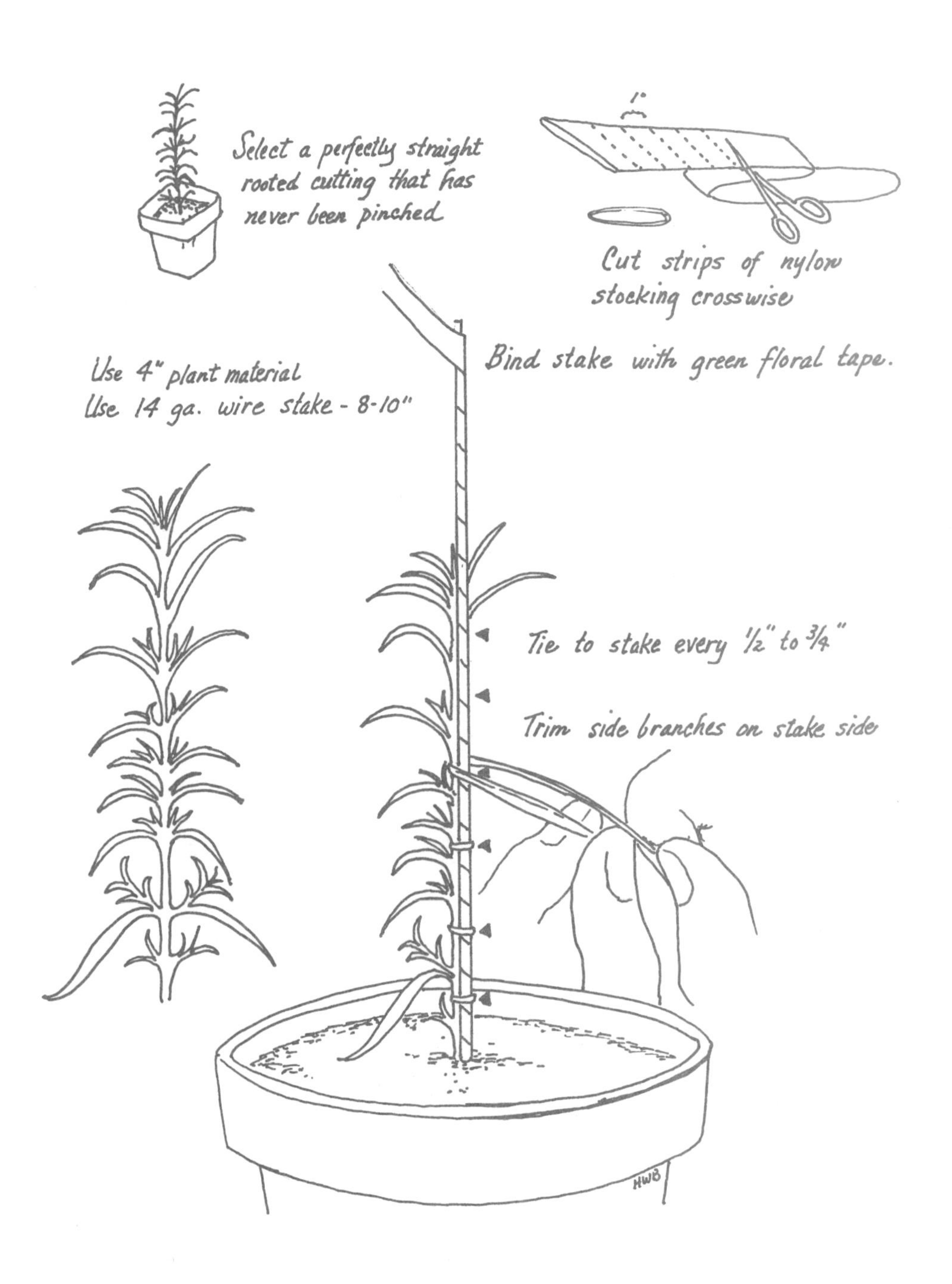
Select a perfectly straight
rooted cutting that has
never been pinched
1"
Cut strips of nylon
stocking crosswise
Use 4" plant material
Use 14 ga. wire stake - 8-10"
Bind stake with green floral tape.
Tie to stake every 1/2" to 3/4"
Trim side branches on stake side
HWB

and white blooms cover the plant.

Herbal standards are pleasant to prune, as fragrant oils cover one's fingers with marvelous scents. Rosemary is a favorite herbal standard. There are over forty rosemaries available. It is best to use a short-leaf rosemary that is not subject to fungal infections, and one that grows upright.

Lavenders make fine standards but are slightly more difficult to grow than rosemaries. Scented geraniums are great candidates for standards if a variety with a compact growth habit and small leaves is chosen. Scented geraniums always have to be staked, as their trunks are not truly woody.

Creating a Standard

TO CREATE a standard, choose a perfectly straight, rooted cutting on which the growing tip has never been pinched. If one specifies on an order to an herb supply house that the plant requested will be used for a standard, they will most likely ship a straight plant. If a plant with several stems is shipped, it is possible to take one of those stems for training or to take a cutting of the straightest branch, root it in perlite, and use it instead.

Start with four inches of straight plant material. Use a four-inch pot and center the young plant directly in the middle. Choose a 14-gauge wire stake, about eight to ten inches in length, and tie the plant leader to the stake. All leaves must be removed between the leader and the stake, as even the smallest stem or leaf will create a bulge in the future stem of that plant.

It is best to tie the plant to the stake, using strips of nylon stockings, cut crosswise. Nylon has some give to it, if not stretched to its limit. String, raffia, Twist-ems, etc. are more rigid and allow the designer no freedom to forget those ties as the plant grows. They act as tourniquets and will leave marks on the stem if not checked frequently and retied as necessary.

Wire stakes come in many lengths and diameters. Start with 14-gauge and work up to 8-gauge. The stakes should be absolutely straight and wrapped with green floral tape which is aesthetically pleasing, and is sticky so that the ties will adhere to the stake. The tape also serves to keep metal stakes cooler in the hot sun, thereby avoiding burning plant stems.

Detail showing tying of main stem with side branches left on non-stake side for photosynthesis (drawing shows grey or variegated plant material)

Replace original stake with one twice as long when the leader reaches top of original stake. Retie every inch.

Attach a "corkscrew" of wire to the base of the *lower* gauged stakes for stability. They can be fashioned from wire or by welding three supports to the base (Christmas-tree fashion). Roots will grow around it. Without support, the longer, heavier stakes will wobble and disturb the roots. When the standard is mature, the wire stake can be cut away at soil level if a corkscrew or supports have been secured to the bottom.

If the gardener is not going to show this standard in a flower show and is not fussy about the looks of a slightly crooked stem, using a plastic bamboo stake is adequate. Casual tying with air spaces between the stem and stake is acceptable. Do not use natural bamboo stakes or other wooden stakes as they tend to rot at the soil level.

After the leader has been tied to the stake every one-half to three-quarters of an inch, trim all side branches. An inch of side branches and leaves growing out from the stem is needed for photosynthesis—the process whereby plants form carbohydrates (food) in their chlorophyll-containing cells. If working with grey or variegated plants in a hot and humid climate, leave generous amounts of side stems and leaves on the plants. Especially if working with a plant with variegated foliage, such as variegated Prince Rupert geranium, water only when the soil is dry, and move the plant into bright light, out of the sun during hot humid weather.

Care in Pruning

IT IS IMPORTANT to understand how the pruning of terminal buds—the growing buds on the ends of all shoots—stimulates the growth of other buds along the plant stems. In the leaf axil where each leaf stalk is attached to the stem, there hides an axillary lateral bud capable of becoming a branch. In a young plant, *auxins* (hormones) are present in the terminal bud. They tell the bud to keep growing and inhibit the axillary buds from breaking dormancy. When the tip is pruned away, removing the terminal bud, these axial buds and others lying dormant on the stem, called *adventitious* buds will sprout. Pruning may have to be repeated several times in order to force all of the dormant buds to grow and become branches.

Once the plant leader reaches the top of the stake, cut off all the ties and remove the stake. Take another stake twice as long as the present stem, push it into the soil to the bottom of the container (on the side where all the side shoots and leaves were removed), and tie again. The

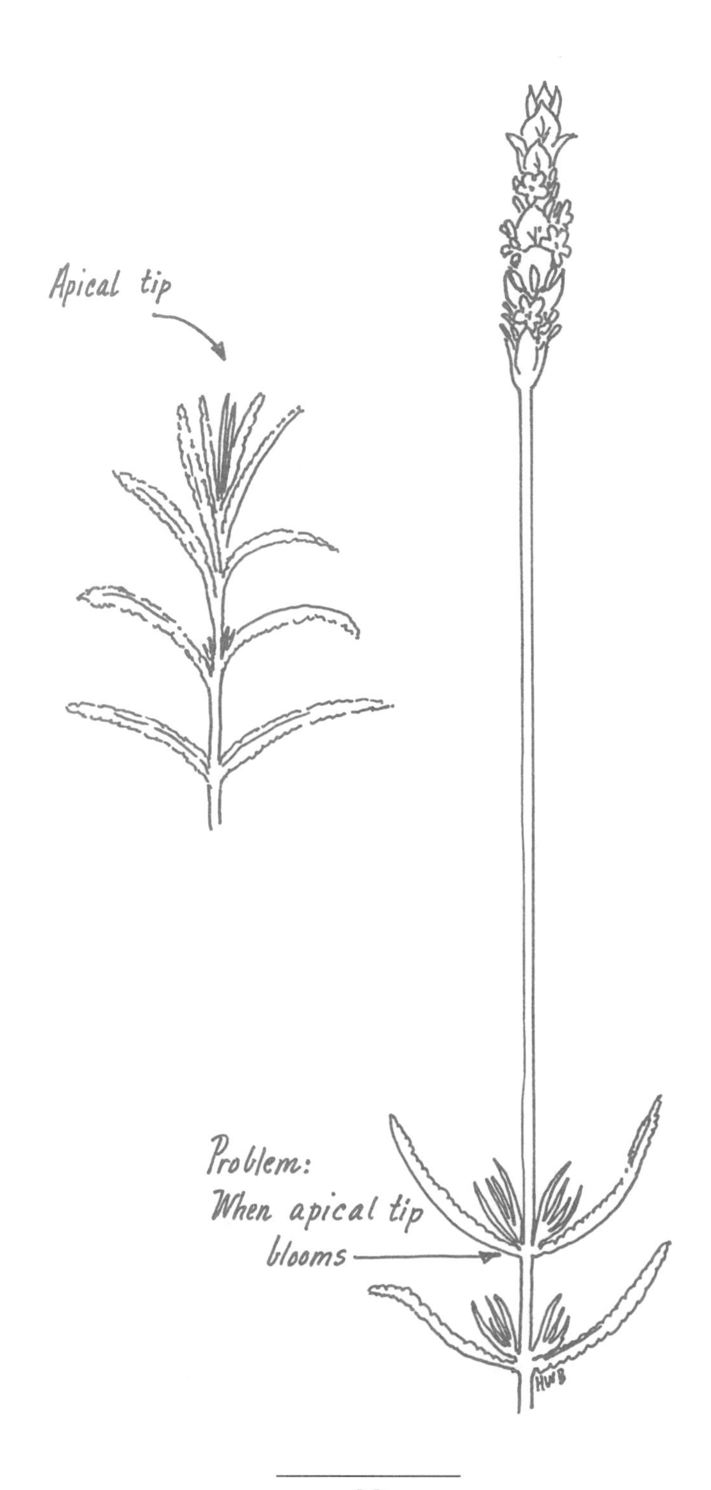
Apical tip
Problem:
When apical tip
blooms
HWB

portion of the stem that has become woody needs very soft ties, at one-inch intervals.

Be very careful with the vegetative tip of the leader. Do not try to cut away leaves from the last half inch to an inch, as one runs the risk of cutting the growing tip itself. If the growing tip does become severed, that will be the terminal of the standard and the head must be developed. A head developed at any height can be added onto by taking one central branch and making it a leader in order to develop a second head. Once that head is developed the procedure may be repeated for yet a third head. Such topiaries are called "poodles."

When the growing stem reaches the desired height, it should be pinched off.

To grow the head, allow two to four pairs of side branches to develop at the terminal. Cut away all other leaves and side branches that have been photosynthesizing on the stem—their work is over. With wire cutters, cut away that portion of the metal stake that runs through the head. As all the growth has been removed from the stem where it comes in contact with the stake, if the stake is left in place up in the developing head, no shoots will grow there. As maturity occurs, there will be a decided hole in the head on the stake side if the stake is not cut away. This is not possible with "poodles," where the stake must be left in place to develop another leader and head. The total height of the standard may be anywhere from several inches to several feet. The height will depend on the size of the leaves, the intended use for the mature standard, and the amount of room available in the winter quarters.

Sometimes the apical tip of an herb in training will bloom. Once this occurs it becomes extremely difficult to get more apical growth so that the stem can continue. One can form the head at that juncture or one can take a side-growing shoot and skillfully bend it to become the new leader, cutting away the flower stalk and the other side-growing shoots.

With some herbs, such as scented-leaf geraniums, it is possible to cultivate a good straight stem from a sucker shoot. This will grow out of the root ball. Use it for a new leader, tying it to a stake as described. Repot this new leader, cutting away all old plant material and reducing the root ball.

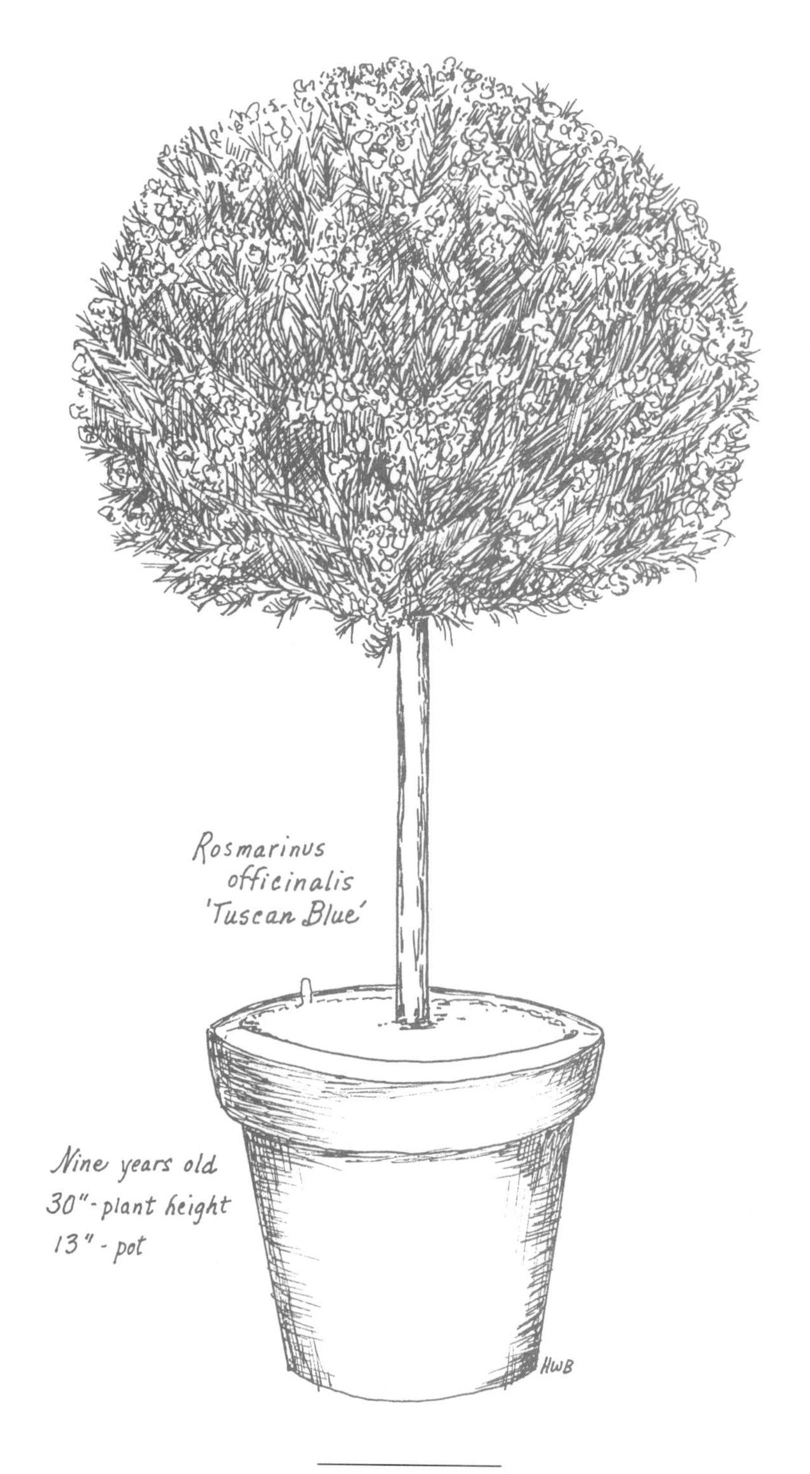
Rosmarinus
officinalis
'Tuscan Blue'
Nine years old
30"- plant height
13" - pot
HWB

Indoors or Out?

IT IS VERY DIFFICULT to winter-over large standards in the average home. A greenhouse will provide the required conditions: light, cool temperature, proper air circulation, and enough heat to keep the temperature above freezing. Rosemaries wintered in a greenhouse will often bloom all fall and/or winter.

All standards and most plants do best if they are put outside in summer where all the requisite growing conditions exist: sufficient sunlight, breezes, heat, and adequate rainfall (excluding California and desert areas of the western United States). In areas that have high winds, standards need protection because they are top heavy. (See the section entitled "Wind" in Chapter 1: The Secrets of Growing.)

At all times of the year it is important to rotate plant containers one quarter turn at least twice a week to develop a symmetrical head. Always turn in a clockwise direction.

Continuing Care and Artistry

PRUNING IS ESSENTIAL for a fine head—a compact crown made up of many short branches. Cut the stems after every two nodes of growth. Allow the lower part of the head to become wider than the top in order to receive sufficient sunlight (this same principle applies to growing a hedge). Most herbs bloom in the summer. If blooms are desired in the late summer or fall, prune the head up until two months before the desired flowering. Fall pruning is not recommended for plants that remain outdoors or go into cold greenhouses, as nutrients stored in their branches and leaves are needed for winter dormancy.

A complete pruning of a head should be done one month before a show.

Gibberellic acid, available at garden centers, may be used to increase the growth rate of standards. Follow the directions on the label carefully. A standard will take up to two years to form and another two years to fully mature. The gibberellic acid will lengthen the spaces between lateral buds, but shorten the time necessary to grow a mature standard.

Geranium standards are short-lived as they do not develop true woody stems. They take from one to two years to produce, are decorative for

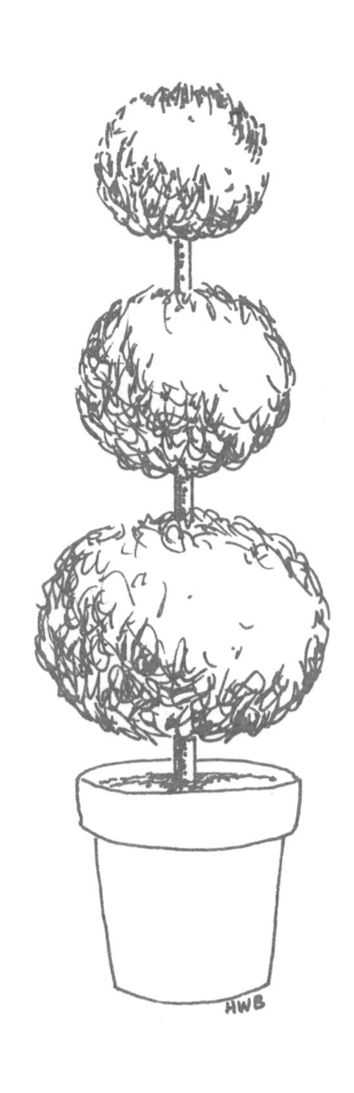

Myrtus communis 'Microphylla'

about three years, then lose their attractiveness. If a geranium head is made up of long branches it should be protected, as they can snap in a strong wind.

Cultivating an herbal standard is creating a form of living art—one's work is never finished. Watering, fertilizing, pruning, removing dead leaves, rootpruning, and repotting are necessary throughout the life of the plant. But what a joyous reward a finished standard brings.

Poodles, or Multitiered Standards

POODLES (multitiered standards) feature three or five (odd numbers) heads developed along a single straight stem. In order to create a poodle, allow side growth to develop along the stem of the standard at intervals where the balls are to grow. Through constant pinching of the growing tips (usually every two sets of leaves) compact tufts will develop. Allow the lower tufts to grow larger than the upper to promote a more interesting and pleasing shape.

Poodles can also be developed in stages. Grow a standard with a short stem, perhaps five to seven inches from the soil line. When the head of the plant is mature, tie one central branch to a stake and allow it to grow several inches. At the desired height pinch this leader and develop a second head. In a year or so the woody stem will no longer need staking. A third head may be cultivated in a similar fashion. This is a more time-consuming method of develop multitiered standards, but it is the one that I have used successfully.

Herbs to Use for Standards

Aloysia triphylla—lemon verbena
Cuphea hyssopifolia—elfin herb, false heather*
Helichrysum italicum ssp. *siitalicum* 'Nana'—dwarf curry plant
Helichrysum petiolatum—licorice plant
Laurus nobilis—sweet bay
Lavandula dentata—French lavender
Lavandula stoechas—French lavender, Spanish lavender

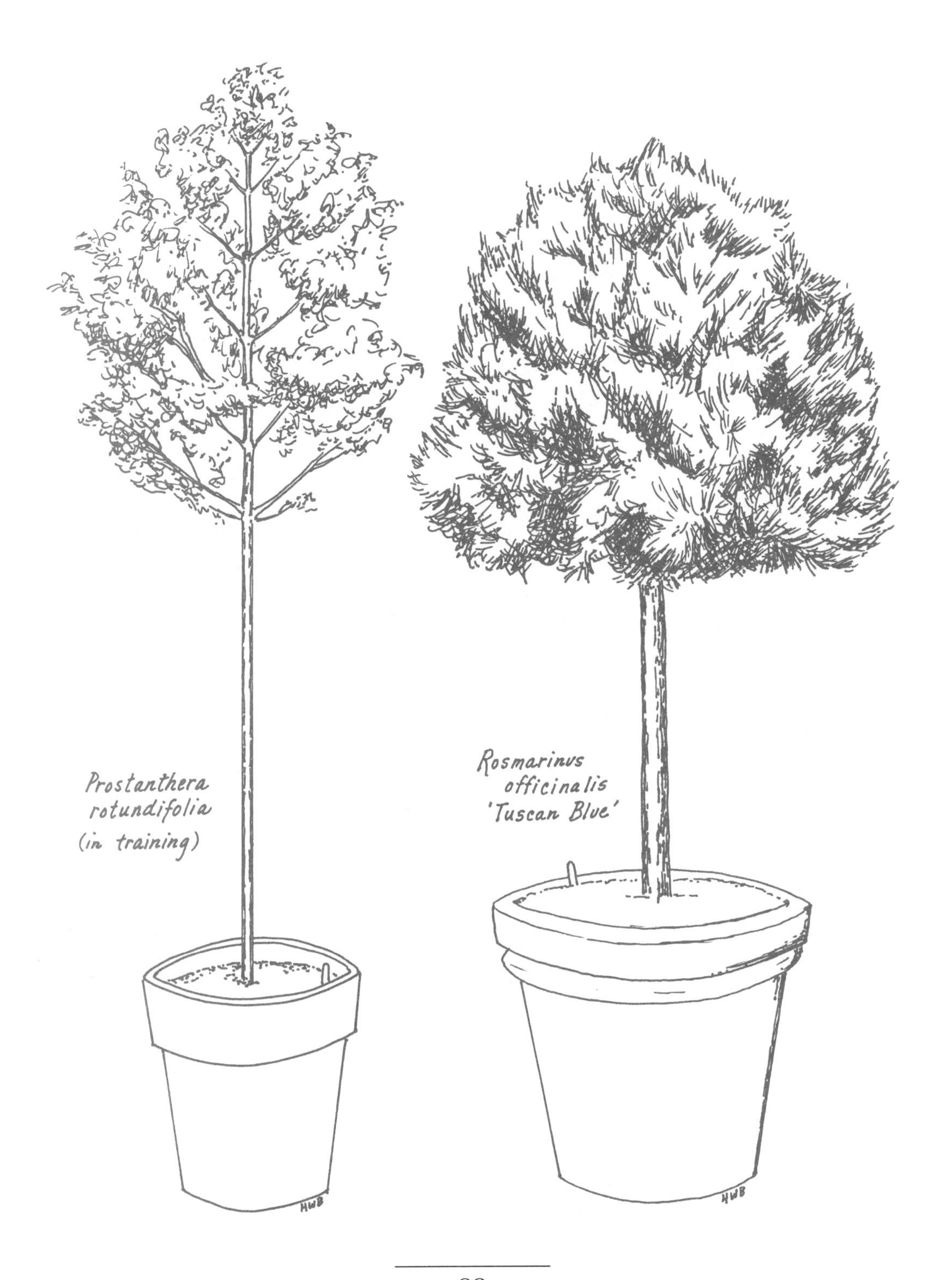
Prostanthera
rotundifolia
(in training)
Rosmarinus
officinalis
'Tuscan Blue'
HWB
HWB

Lavandula x intermedia 'Grosso'—lavandin**
Leptospermum scoparium 'Roseum'—Australian tea rose, New Zealand tea tree
Lippia dulcis—sweet herb
Myrtus communis 'Microphylla'—dwarf myrtle, German myrtle
Myrtus communis 'Microphylla Variegata'—variegated dwarf myrtle
Pelargonium crispum—lemon geranium
Pelargonium grossulariodes—gooseberry-leaved geranium
Pelargonium 'Prince Rupert Variegated'—variegated Prince Rupert geranium
Pelargonium graveolens 'Little Gem'—little gem geranium (larger leaved)
Pelargonium x nervosum—lime geranium (larger leaved)
Pelargonium radens 'Dr. Livingston'—Dr. Livingston geranium
Pelargonium scabrum—apricot geranium (larger leaved)
Pelargonium x scarboroviae (P. cv. 'Countess of Scarborough')—strawberry geranium
Pelargonium torento—ginger geranium (larger leaved)
Poliomintha longiflora—Mexican oregano
Prostanthera rotundifolia—Australian mint bush (grows rapidly)
Rosmarinus officinalis 'Arp'—Arp rosemary***
Rosmarinus officinalis 'Kenneth Prostrata'—Kenneth prostrate rosemary
Rosmarinum officinalis 'Logee Blue'—Logee blue rosemary
Rosmarinus officinalis 'Prostratus'—prostrate rosemary
Rosmarinus officinalis 'Tuscan Blue'—tuscan blue rosemary (upright)
Santolina chamaecyparissus—grey lavender cotton
Thymus argenteus—silver thyme (treat the leader gently)

*Horticulturist Cyrus Hyde takes three shoots, braids them, and makes a fine standard from cuphea.

**This is a cross between *L. angustifolia* and *L. latifolia*. Used in France for commercial production, if planted in the garden it is hardy to 0° F. It will thrive in a raised bed mulched with one or two inches of sand that does not retain water, thereby decreasing the risk of fungal infections.

***As a garden plant, Arp is hardy from 0° F to −10°F, mulched with sand.

Rosmarinus officinalis
'Tuscan Blue'

CHAPTER 5

Tying Herbs onto a Topiary Frame

HERBAL TOPIARIES, tied to a frame, are the most exciting and creative form of topiary art. Limited only by one's imagination, the finished topiaries are very beautiful and have the potential of being alive with movement.

In this type of topiary, plant material is tied onto a wire skeleton, which can be made into any desired shape—globes, stick people, circles, corkscrews, and other geometric forms, as well as silhouettes of trees and animals (particularly birds), or imaginative free forms.

The Wire Form

WIRE FORMS may be made from #9 galvanized wire, which very strong hands can bend. Pieces should be soldered where they cross or meet, or florist wire can be used to bind two wire pieces together. Covering the entire form with sticky green floral tape not only makes tying easier but is aesthetically more pleasing.

The molded wire form is placed on top of a container of soil, anchored by several supporting wires going down into the pot. The herbs are

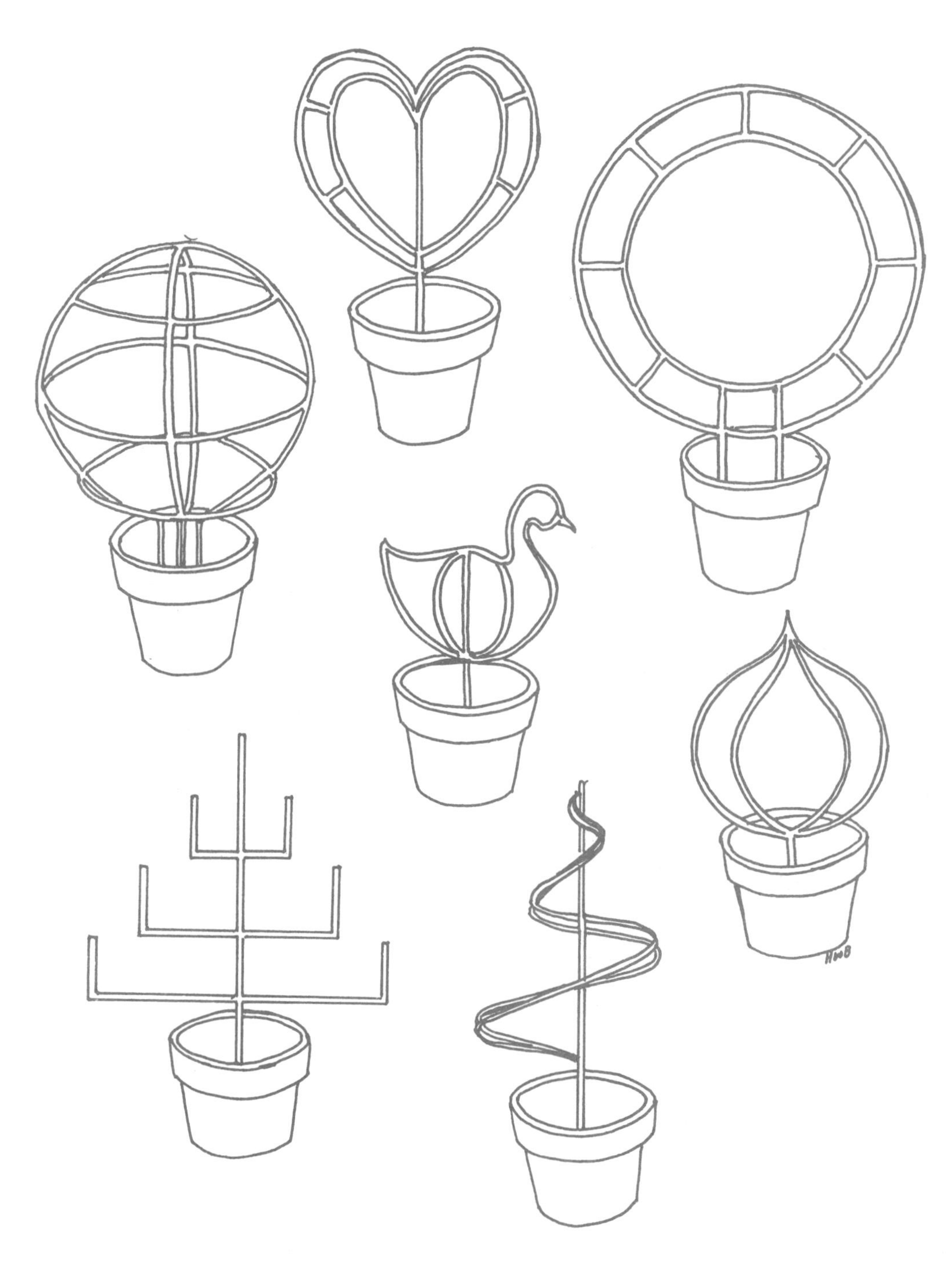

Assorted frames for tied topiary

grown in the container with their leaders tied every one-half inch to the outside portion of the form, following the outline of the wire. Cut away all side branches unless they are needed for another section of the form. When the entire wire form is covered, side branches may be developed to thicken the design, two leaf nodes at a time.

The Plant Leader

A LEADER, GROWING UP FROM THE SOIL, is needed for each line of the form that comes in contact with the soil. The wire form must have a corkscrew at its base or some other means of stabilizing it in the pot of soil. In turn, the leader(s) will develop roots that will stabilize the corkscrew and prevent the form from wobbling.

To tie the leaders to the form, use nylon stocking strips, cut crosswise about one-half inch wide. Cut the stocking at the foot (exclude the heel) and work up the leg. The elasticity of these ties will prevent girdling of the leader should the herbal artist forget to check the ties each week or go on vacation.

Ties may be removed when the plant material becomes woody and strong. Leaders must be molded to the form during their vegetative state, when they are soft and pliable. Should a leader become severed, it is possible to develop a new one; the resulting "lump" will be disguised by growth as the plant matures.

Leaders should always be on the outer side of the wire form, and knots from the ties should be on the inside. Every week during active growth the new growth should be tied down and the old ties removed unless they are not girdling and have room to stretch. Ties do not have to be replaced on those sections of the leaders that have become woody.

Leaves or stems on the side of the leader touching the form must be removed. No ties should cover a leaf or its petiole; tie just above a leaf or set of leaves.

It is not a good procedure to twine the leader around a form. It looks sloppy and detracts from the beauty of this finished product.

Creating a Double Circle Topiary

IN CREATING a double circle topiary, more than one leader is necessary. In this case, a larger and a smaller circle are connected by pieces of straight wire soldered at the connections. The anchoring mechanism should be attached at either side of the larger circle, with the supports close enough to each other to fit into a six- or eight-inch pot, depending on the scale and proportion of the frame to the container. Either two (preferably) or four rooted cuttings may be used at each side of the pot (disguising the supports for the frame), then trained onto the circles, one or two leaders for each circle, one being the slower method but producing a finer finished specimen.

Cut the two leaders when they meet, if two leaders have been used for one circle. Allow the resulting branching from the leaf axils to produce two sets of leaves, then cut again. Each snipping of a branch will produce two branches. These two can then be snipped to produce four branches, those four will produce eight, and so on.

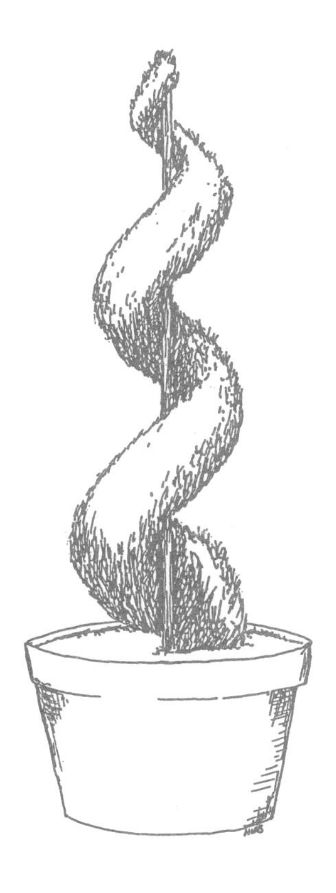

There is another way to create a spiral which I have not tried. Using a dowel or broomstick at least one inch in diameter, fasten a brightly colored adhesive tape to the top and wind it down the stake in a spiral manner. Wrap a strong leader of plant material to the dowel, following the line of the colored tape. Encourage branching along the entire stem. When the main stem becomes woody, and the spiral is near completion, the stake may be removed.

Keep in mind that major plant growth occurs during the warm months, so keep topiaries outdoors and in full sun. Double pot mulching with pebbles between the two pots, and using pebbles as a top dressing, will help to prevent topiaries from tipping over in the wind.

A completed herbal topiary will have woody leaders that have taken the shape of the molded wire form. With some herbs it will be possible to cut away the wire form.

It is difficult to estimate how long these finished plants will last. Forgetting to water or to root-prune and repot with fresh soil at least once a year—or an "act of God"—could cause their demise. But with continuous nurturing and pruning these plants can last several years.

A Plan for a Tied Topiary

Assemble the equipment needed:

wire form (You can make your own. Use #9 galvanized wire. Be sure that the form has a corkscrew base that will fit into a six-inch clay pot. If the form is large, with two corkscrew bases, use an eight-inch pot.)
plastic florist tape
plant(s) with straight leader (s)
six- or eight-inch pot
plastic screening
soil
nylon stocking ties
iris scissors
chopstick
pebbles for top dressing

1. Cover the wire form completely with plastic floral tape from the top of the form to the soil line.

2. Place plastic screening over the drainage hole of the pot.

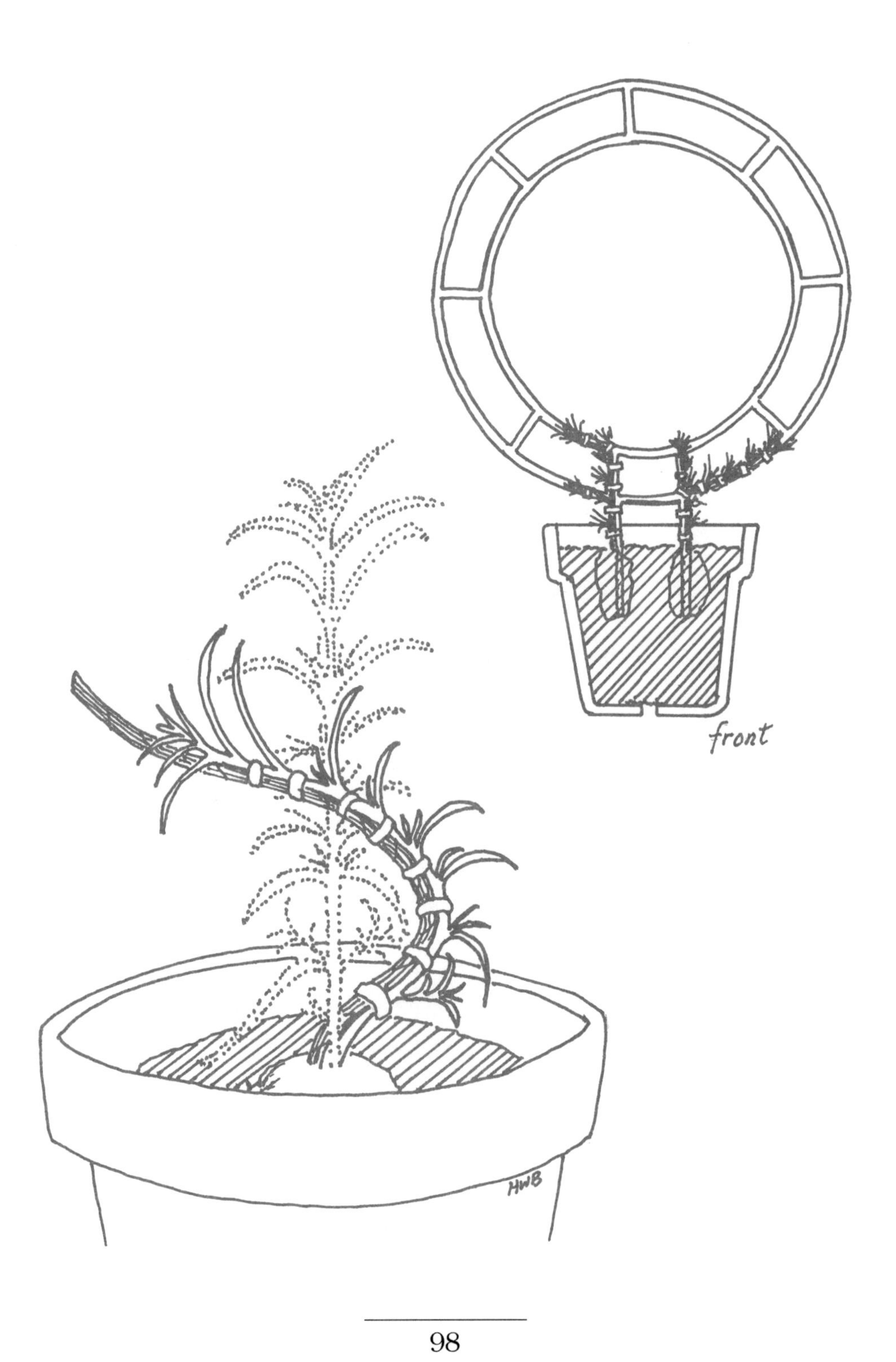
front
HWB

3. Arrange the plant and wire form in the pot. The leader(s) should be set directly next to the ascending portion of the form at the soil line.

4. Center the form and the plant(s). Fill the pot with soil and tamp the soil down around the leader and wire form with a chopstick. If a circular form is used, the lowest part of the circle should sit two inches above the soil line and one inch above the lip of the pot. This will allow for future growth in good scale and proportion to the container. This point is important for I have seen many which were started with the circle at the soil line—they will never look right.

5. Start tying the leader to the outer side of the wire form. There should be one leader tied to each line of the form at the soil level. Tie each nylon stocking tie into a square knot, trimming the ends to leave a small, neat double knot. (The knots should align on the inside of the form.) The ties should be loose enough to insert a toothpick between the plant and the wire form and tight enough to prevent the ties from sliding.

6. Plant the herbs directly next to the form, removing any leaves or stems that might make a bulge by growing in between the plant and the form. Tie every half-inch between leaf nodes, making certain not to cover any of the leaves or petrioles. Prune away any plant shoots that are not part of the design.

7. Examine the plant ties weekly. If the ties can be pushed up or down they are not too tight. If they are girdling the leader like a tourniquet, remove them (preferably with iris scissors) and retie. Check the leader for bumps. Make sure it is growing close to the form. Tie down new vegetative growth at the apex, being very careful not to injure this soft tissue as the leaves are cut off. It is best not to touch the terminal inch.

8. Cut off the leader when it has grown the desired length.

9. Branches may be developed to cover any sides of the form not covered by a leader. These branches should also be tied. Cut their growing tips once they reach another leader and are no longer needed.

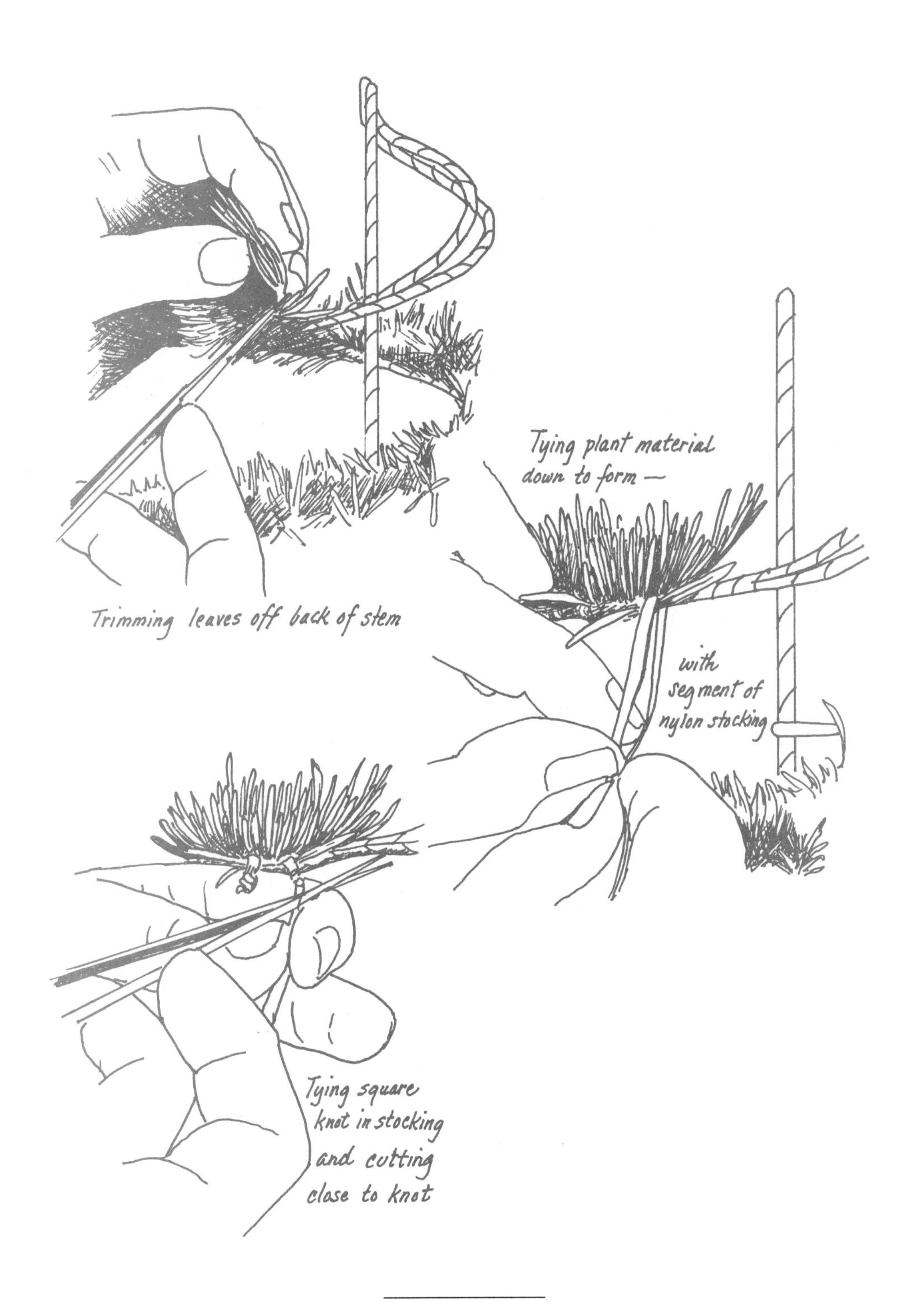
Trimming leaves off back of stem
Tying plant material
down to form —
with
segment of
nylon stocking
Tying square
knot in stocking
and cutting
close to knot

Plants To Use for Tied Topiary

Myrtus communis 'Microphylla'—dwarf myrtle
Myrtus communis 'Microphylla Variegata'—variegated dwarf myrtle
Rosmarinus officinalis—rosemary*
Rosmarinus officinalis 'Alida Hyde'—Alida Hyde prostrate rosemary
Rosmarinus officinalis 'Blue Boy'—blue boy rosemary
Rosmarinus officinalis 'Lockwoodi de Forest'—Lockwood de Forest rosemary

*Either upright or prostrate varieties, small-leaved, are preferable.

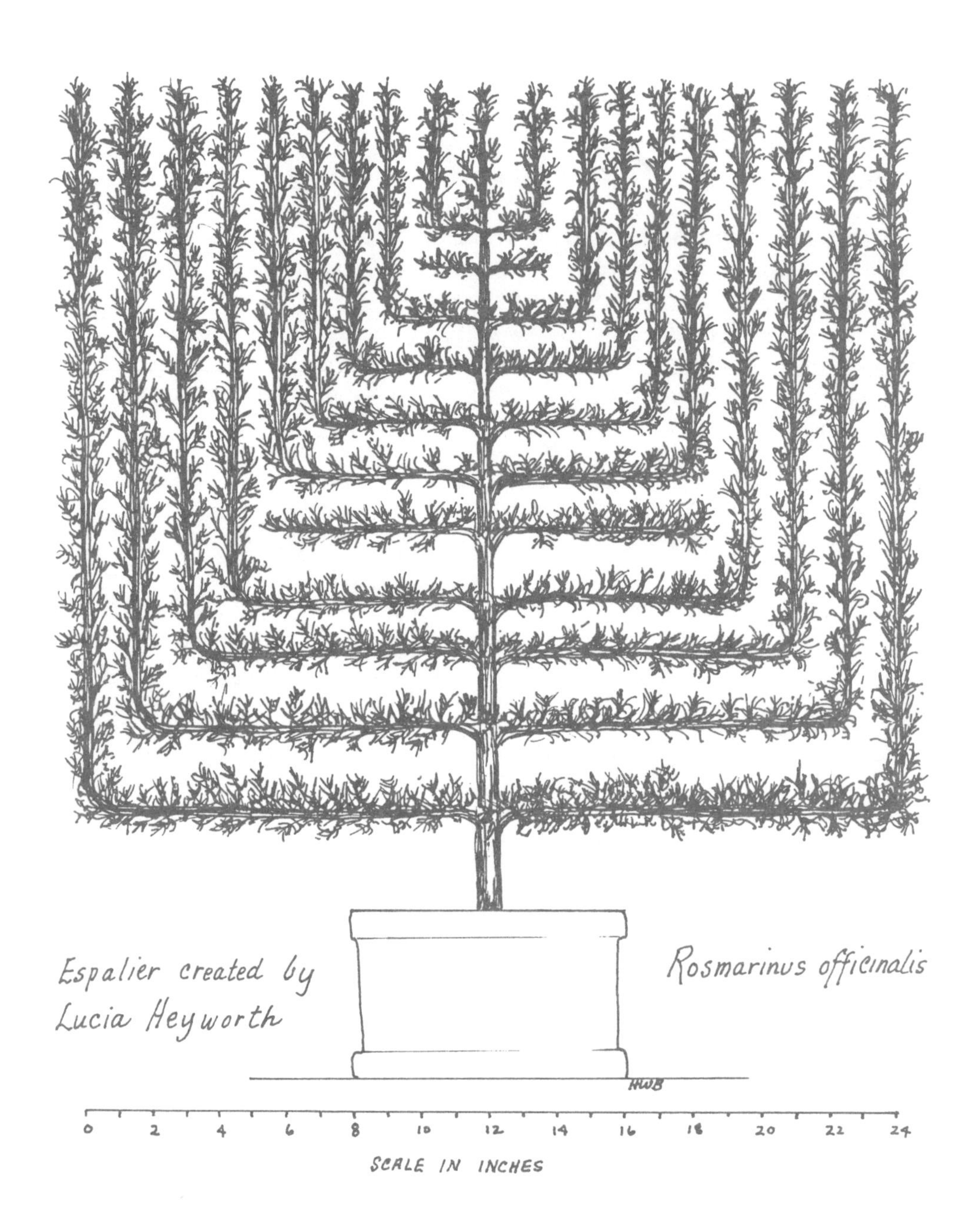
Espalier created by
Lucia Heyworth
Rosmarinus officinalis
HWB
0
2
4
6
8
10
12
14
16
18
20
22
24
SCALE IN INCHES

CHAPTER 6

Espalier, Using Herbs

ESPALIER is the art of growing a plant in one plane, against a wall, trellis, or other flat support. To be viewed from one side only, an espalier can be trained in the most confined spaces—against a house wall, a balcony fence, a screen on a terrace, or a garden wall—providing there is ample sunlight. An espalier can also be trained in a freestanding container with its own wire support.

In Europe, fruit trees are often grown espalier style against a wall. An espalier not only saves space but growing a plant against a wall will also protect fruit blossoms from the damages of a late spring frost as well as providing warmth for ripening fruit.

Cultivating an espalier requires weekly attention during the growing season. In southern sections of the United States, herbs can be espaliered outside in a permanent location. How charming an outdoor myrtle espalier can be, with a profusion of white flowers in summer followed by clusters of black berries! Hardy to 25°F and evergreen, myrtle should have an eastern exposure in climates where the temperature is consistently high to protect it from the baking sun.

For the northern portion of the United States, an herb can be trained

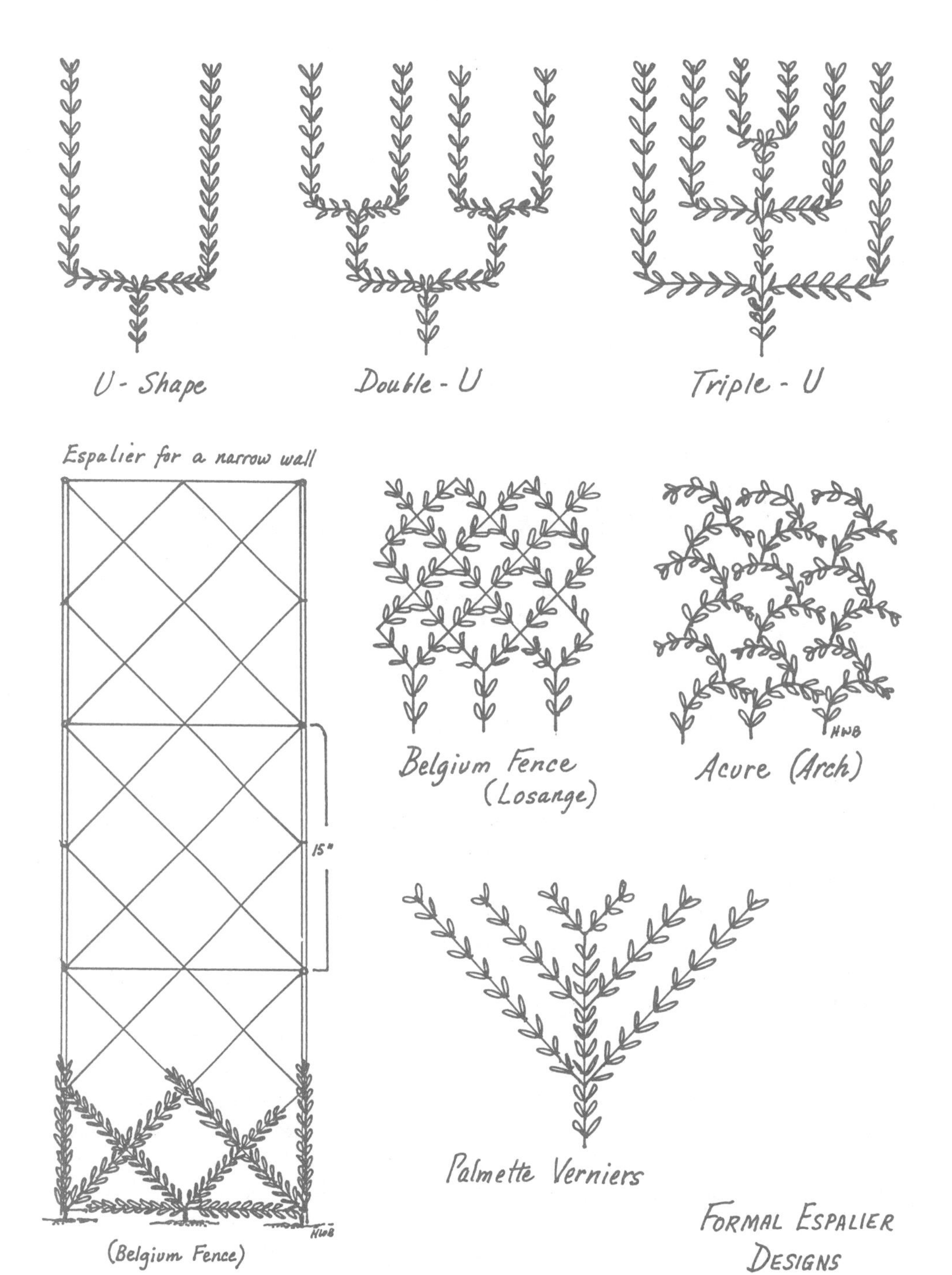

FORMAL ESPALIER DESIGNS

on a piece of hardware cloth that has been secured with wire stakes into a container. Rosemary, lavender, and dwarf myrtle are the best candidates for this kind of espalier.

Formal or Informal?

THERE ARE TWO distinct patterns of espalier design from which to choose—formal and informal. Formal patterns feature symmetrical growth and may appeal to those who prefer more symmetrical lines. Informal patterns allow for freer expression and, should a leader die, a greater margin for error. A formal pattern could be permanently marred by any accident.

The basic designs for formal espaliers are upright, diagonal and horizontal cordons (a single trunk), and a variant called the horizontal-T; U-shaped espaliers and variations known as the double-U, and triple-U; palmette verniers; Belgian fence; losange and acure espaliers, and fans.

Informal espaliers should take the form the plant suggests by the shape and direction of its natural growth. The plant can expand in various upward and outward freeform patterns.

It is best to start an espalier with a young plant while the growth is still pliable. In Europe, branches are trained flat against masonry. In the United States, however, allow for air space between the plant material and a wall that reflects much heat. A wooden trellis or a number of tightly-stretched wires can be constructed to fit onto the wall. The wires can be fixed to the wall with metal dowels implanted in the mortar in a horizontal, vertical, or diagonal fashion depending on the chosen pattern. The branches of the espalier are then tied onto the trellis or to the taut wires.

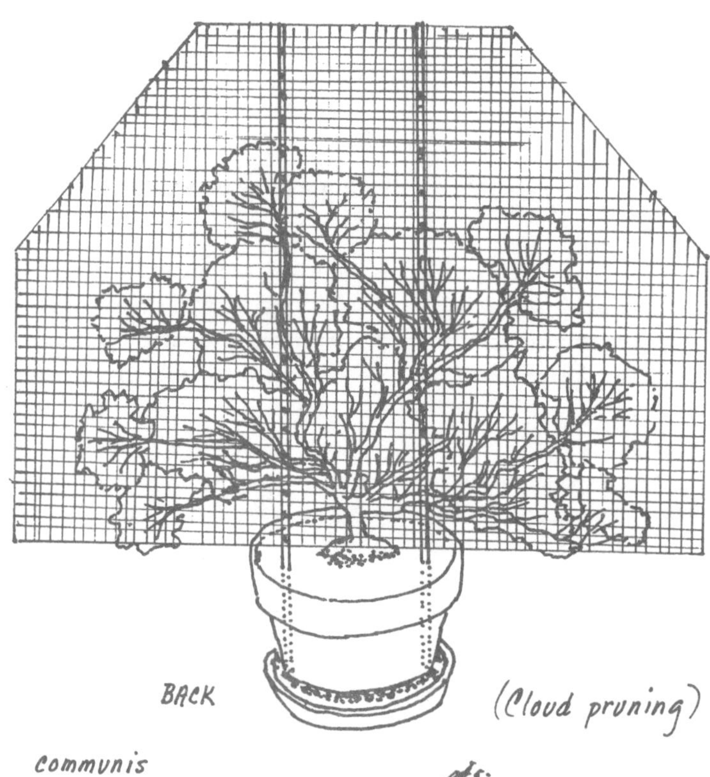
BACK
(Cloud pruning)

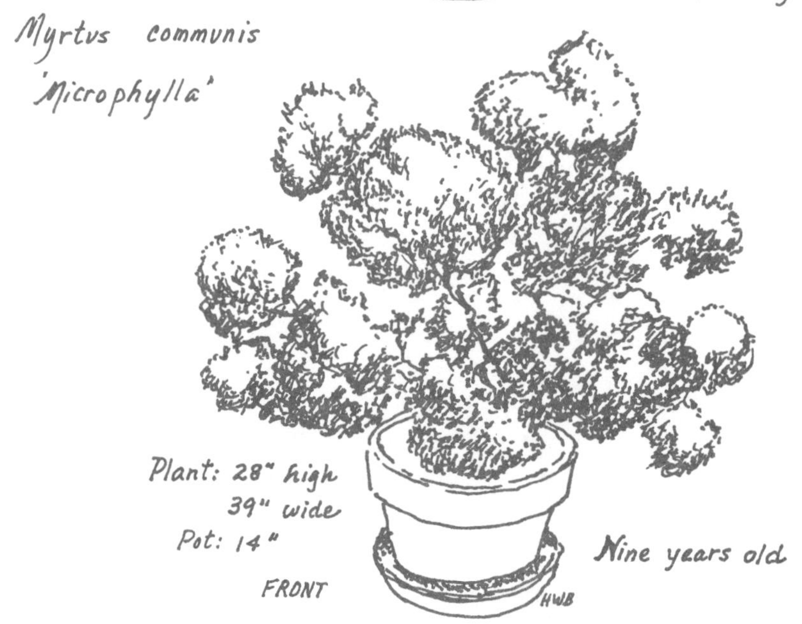
Myrtus communis
'Microphylla'
Plant: 28" high
39" wide
Pot: 14"
FRONT
Nine years old
HWB

A Pattern of Growth

IN GENERAL, a leader and major side branches must be tied to the chosen pattern. Major side branches are called *scaffolds*. They are the part of the framework from which secondary growth will develop. The pattern can be drawn on hardware cloth as well as made with wires or a trellis. All other side branches are removed—only leaves on the viewing side of the plant material are kept. Depending on the scale, when the framework is completed side branching (two leaf nodes at a time) may be allowed to develop. The voids between major branches define the pattern and should be kept.

Cloud pruning is a variant of an informal espalier. In this freestanding style an informal fan-shaped espalier is created. The terminals are allowed to develop heads of side growth and outward growth. Pruning should be done outside on a day when cumulus clouds are overhead, to observe their free form and different depths. This can be "duplicated" with container-grown plant material. Dwarf myrtle is an especially good choice. When several "clouds" are completed, one leader from the top center of each cloud can be chosen and tied down to grow. When the new leaders reach a length equal to that of the original clouds and their stems, then the head of each of these leaders can be grown irregularly for a second group of clouds.

A cloud-pruned topiary should last several decades, providing it receives the necessary care—winter protection, sunlight, watering, fertilizing, pruning, and yearly repotting with root-pruning to retain the same size plant. The backing of this portable topiary may be removed during periods of inactive growth. The branch network viewed from the backside can be most fascinating. The backing has to be replaced and perhaps made larger when new clouds are to be added during periods of active growth.

My *Myrtus communis* 'Microphylla' cloud-pruned topiary is eight years old. The second set of clouds are nearly completed. They do not protrude as far out as the older clouds, which have been growing in an upward and forward direction for many years. It is a very beautiful plant and, because it has not been pruned for several months, it is completely covered with fluffy white blossoms, creating realistic "clouds"!

Perhaps it should be noted that cloud-pruning can also be done in three dimensions, freestanding. This is most frequently seen with junipers, particularly the California juniper.

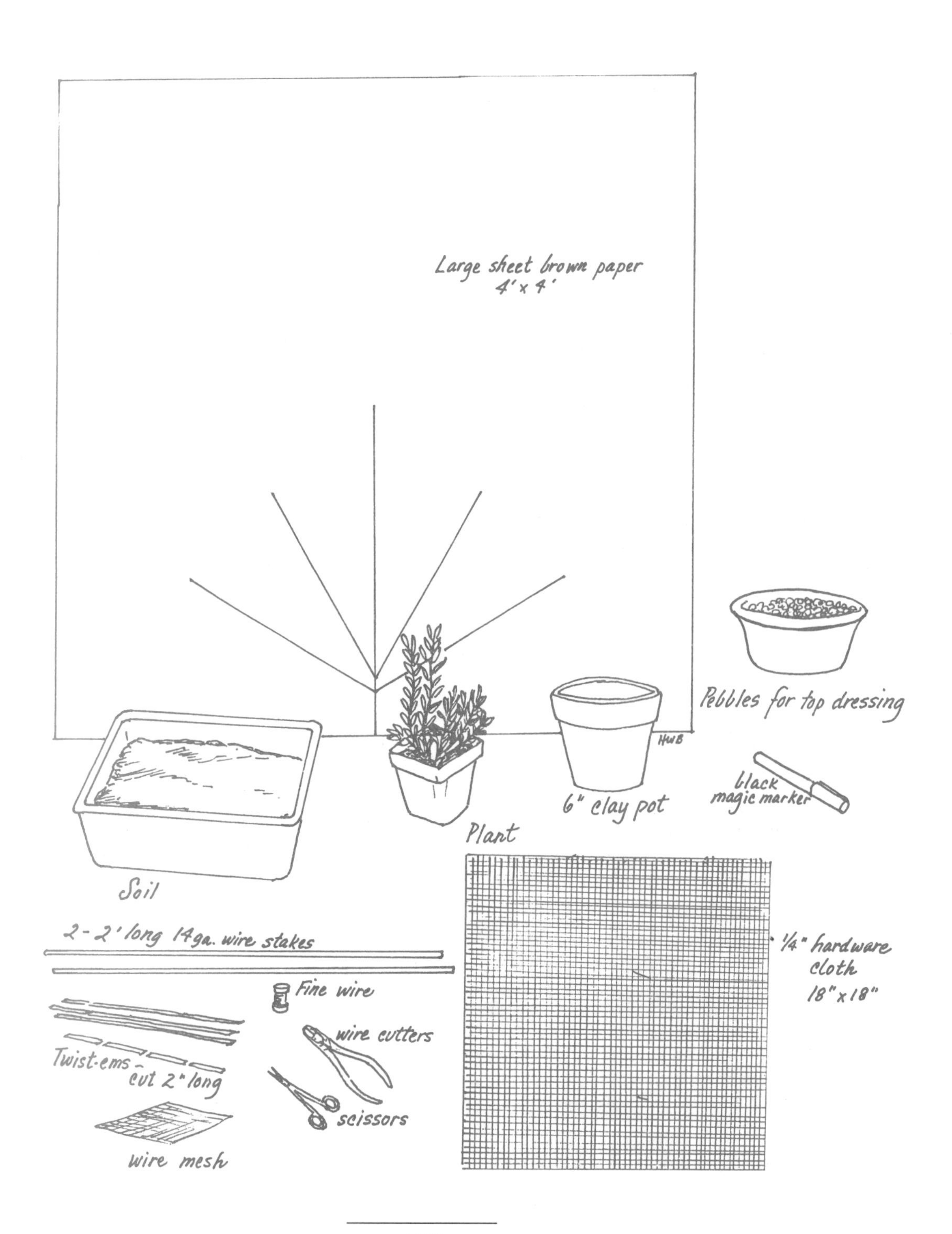
Large sheet brown paper
4'x4'
Pebbles for top dressing
HWB
6" clay pot
black
magic marker
Plant
Soil
2-2' long 14ga. wire stakes
1/4" hardware
cloth
18"x18"
Fine wire
wire cutters
Twist-ems-
cut 2" long
scissors
wire mesh

The wire edges from the hardware cloth behind espaliers will catch on clothing. Those edges can be covered with duct tape. It will prevent lots of pulled threads from knit clothes.

Even in the greenhouse, keep espaliers facing south. In summer mine follow the sun and are turned three times a day to face that great energy source as the earth rotates.

Outside in severe wind storms, large paving bricks can be placed on top of espalier containers and their top dressings to prevent the plants from being blown over.

A Plan for Creating an Herbal Espalier

Assemble the Equipment Needed:

plant (a young, rooted cutting with some branching)
two 14-gauge wire stakes, each 2 feet long
spool of fine wire
hardware cloth (Hardware cloth comes in rolls that are two, three, and four feet wide. The square openings are one-quarter inch or one-half inch.) You will need a piece with one-quarter inch squares, cut to 18″ × 18″.
soil
six-inch standard clay pot
piece of wire mesh
ties (preferably Twist-ems, cut into two-inch pieces)
wire cutters
small iris scissors
brown paper (very large sheet—4′ × 4′)
black magic market
pebbles for top dressing

1. For a portable espalier, it is best to start with a young plant. Give some thought to the espalier's eventual shape. Choose a pattern before starting any espalier. Take a large sheet of brown paper and draw the desired pattern on it.

2. The rolled wire hardware cloth needs to be made flat either with one's hands or by placing it on a cement floor and straightening it with one's feet. Next, take the hardware cloth and cut it one-half to one-third the size of the pattern, representing the first year or so of growth. Place the wire cloth over the paper pattern (again on a flat surface), and transpose the pattern with a black magic marker onto the hardware cloth. Although it is easier to see, white chalk will wash away with watering.

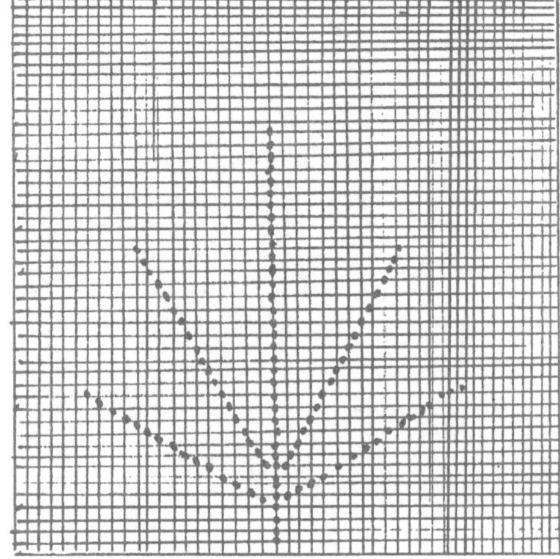

3. Plant the herb in the center of the six-inch clay pot. Select a front side of the plant and cut away all material on the back side of the main branches and trunk.

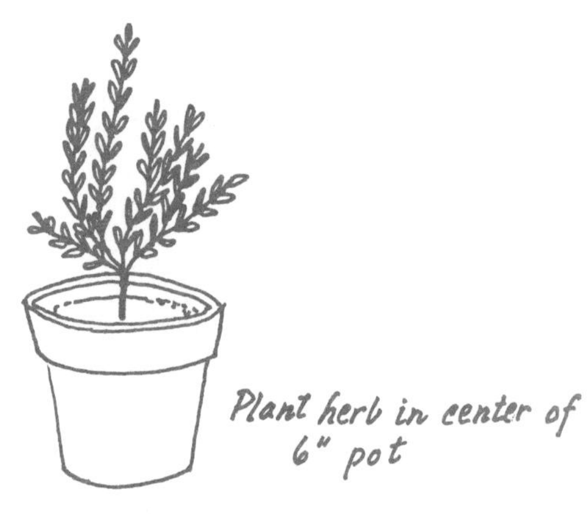

4. Weave the two wire stakes through the hardware cloth from bottom to top, or tie them at intervals to the back side of the hardware cloth with wire. Leave about six inches of stake protruding on the bottom of the form so that the stakes can sit on the floor of the pot. They should be placed three inches apart or one and one-half inches away from bottom dead center of hardware cloth. This compensates for the outward slant of a six-inch pot.

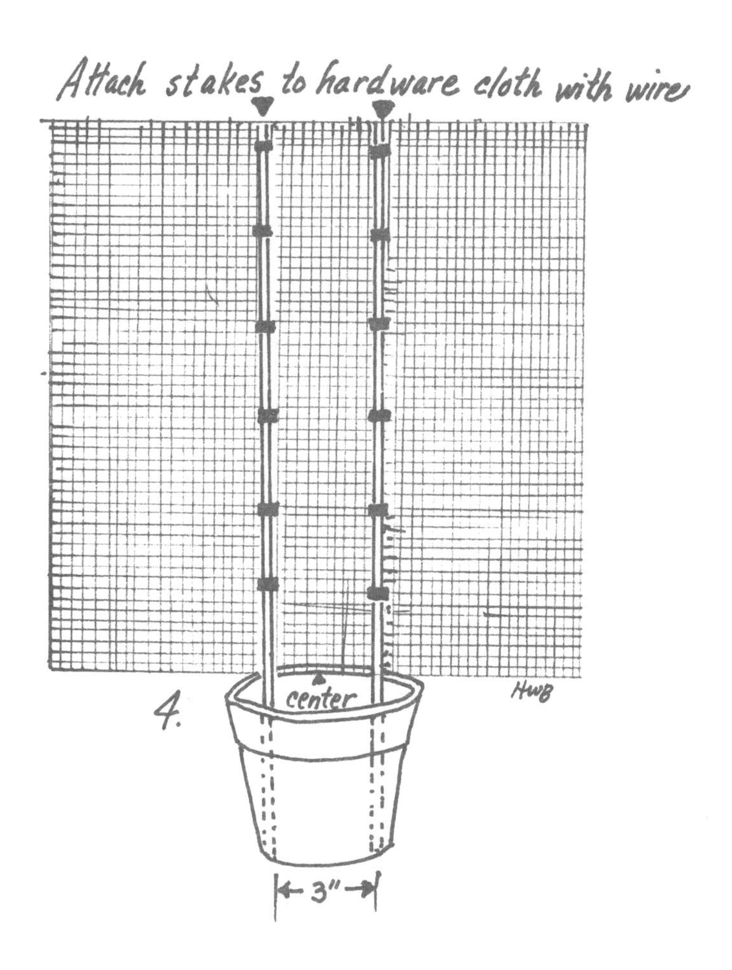

5. Now work the remaining plant material exactly along the lines of the pattern, cutting away all undesired branches at their origin. Work the remaining branches along the pattern, tying them to the hardware cloth with Twist-ems. Twist-ems should be in the back and not too tight, allowing for growth. (Twist-ems are the easiest to poke through hardware cloth and to twist shut in the back.) Nylon stocking pieces can also be used for ties, but these will have to be poked through the hardware cloth with forceps. Tying can also be done with soft twine. Use a tapestry needle and blanket stitch to bring the twine around a stem and attach it to the hardware cloth, taking care not to catch any of the leaves.

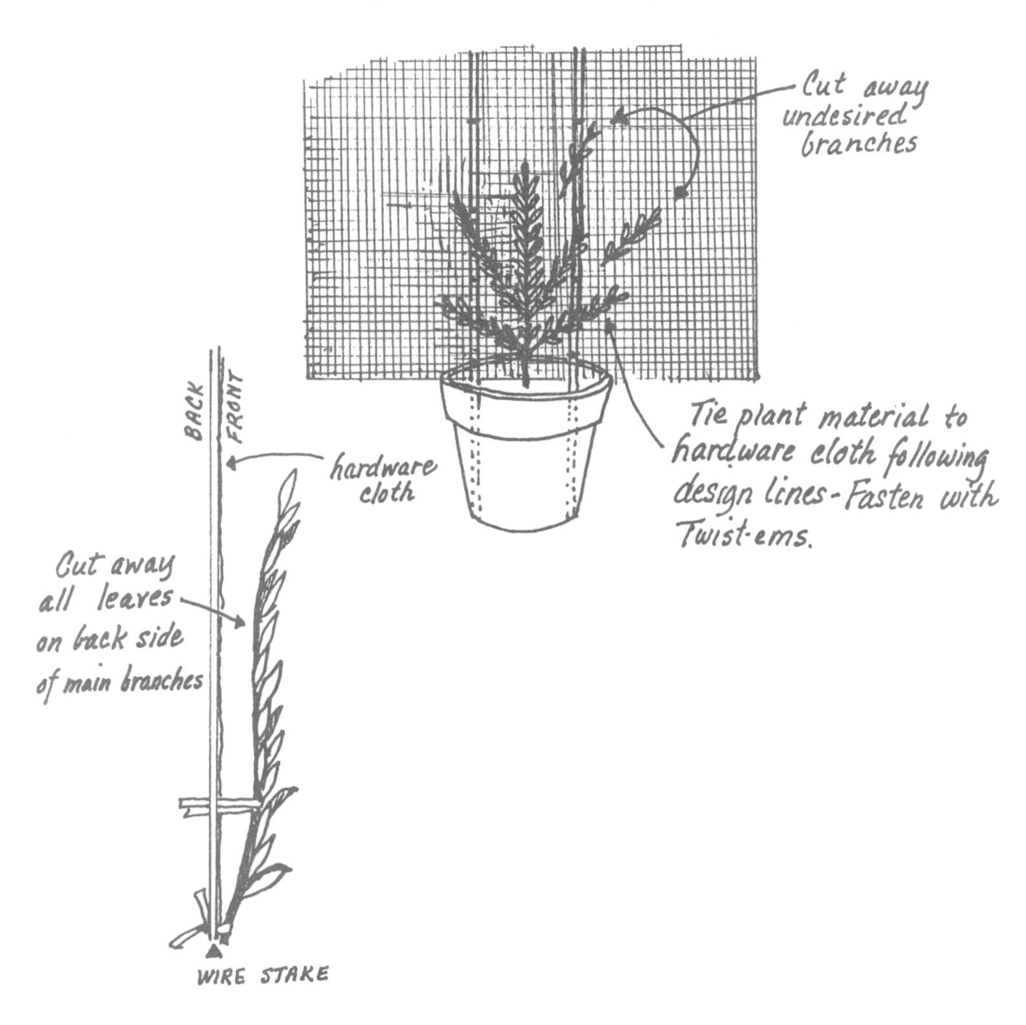

6. Keep training the plant material to the pattern on the hardware cloth. Keep an eye on old ties to see that they are not girdling a leader. Always tie between the leaves. Remove any leaves or lateral buds that develop on the back side of the plant material. (Iris scissors can fit through the hardware cloth to remove them.) The plant should lie flat against the hardware cloth.

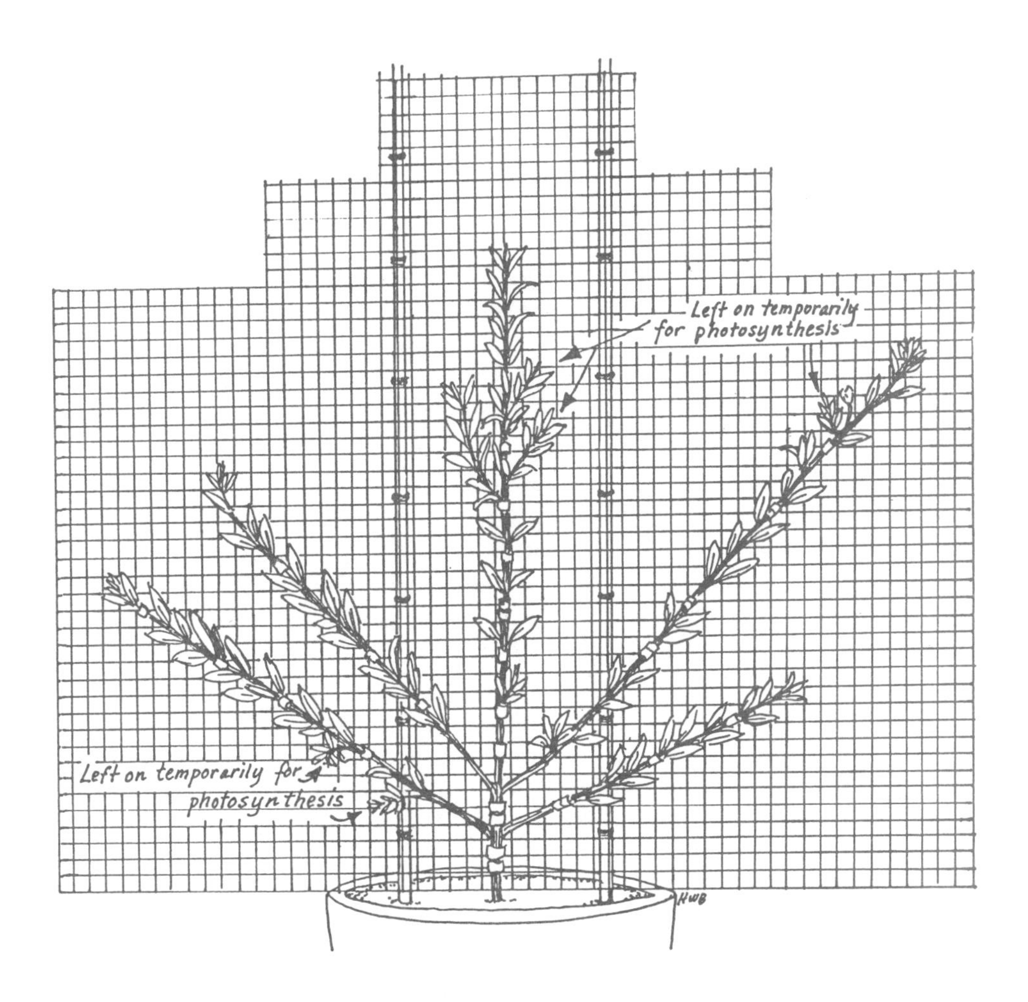

7. Be sure to save the brown paper pattern. When the espaliered plant material outgrows the sheet of quarter-inch hardware cloth, it is time to use a new backing made of the larger cloth with half-inch holes. The new backing should be a piece cut 2½′ × 2½′. Trace more of the pattern on the new, larger piece of hardware cloth from the original 4′ × 4′ piece of brown paper.

8. Again run two wire stakes (this time made of 8-gauge wire) up the cloth, weaving them if possible or tying them on the back with wire. Leave two pieces protruding from the bottom to fit into a new clay pot and rest on its bottom.

9. Remove all the old ties on the espaliered plant with a wire cutter. Remove the old hardware cloth backing and any unnecessary growth and collected debris on the back of the form.

10. Repot the plant; root-prune and add fresh soil. If a standard six-inch pot was used, then the new, larger pot should be a standard eight-inch container. Center the plant, keeping the soil at the same level as it was in the old pot.

11. Have someone hold the plant material forward while you slip the new backing into place directly behind the plant. The stakes supporting the hardware cloth should be on the back side.

12. Tie the plant onto its new backing in the same manner as before. The lower woody portions of the plant will need few ties, but the new vegetative growing ends must be carefully secured.

13. Maintain cultivation and care of the espalier until the growth pattern is finished. For example, when necessary go to a pot one or two sizes larger (ten or twelve inches) with another new piece of hardware cloth, cut to 4′ × 4′. Side branches may be developed to thicken the scaffold branches, but allow only two sets of leaves to grow, then cut. When the scaffold branches have become thick through pruning, this shape can be maintained, provided there is yearly root-pruning and repotting with fresh soil. Espaliers can last a long time. One of my portables is nine years old.

Appropriate Herbs for Espalier

Cuphea hyssopifolia—elfin herb, false heather
Myrthus communis—myrtle
Myrtus communis 'Microphylla'—dwarf myrtle, German myrtle
Myrtus communis 'Microphylla Variegata'—variegated dwarf myrtle
Rosmarinus officinalis—rosemary

Plectranthus amboinicus 'Variegatum'

CHAPTER 7

Herbs in a Moss-covered Hanging Basket

ANGING BASKETS of plants can be as practical as they are decorative. Culinary herbs such as parsley, marjoram, and oregano can be grown in hanging baskets on porches, patios, balconies, or other places where space is limited or might otherwise be wasted. Hanging baskets of nasturtiums surrounding a terrace or porch make a graceful and charming sight. Just be sure the baskets are absolutely secure so they cannot fall and injure someone.

For a grouping of hanging baskets or even for one single basket, moss-covered ones look best. The greenish color (be sure to keep the green side facing out) blends most suitably with plant material. It gives a more natural look.

Selecting and Hanging the Baskets

WIRE BASKETS, available from local garden centers, come with a green or black plastic coating which repels water and prolongs the life of the basket. Sheet moss, also available from garden centers, has to be wet in order to be molded to the insides of the basket. A needle and carpet thread will help secure the top portion of moss to the rim of the basket.

I recommend mixing Grace's Metromix #350 or #360 for soil because of its light weight. It would be wise to include polymers according to the directions, remembering that they will increase the bulk of the soil by about twenty percent.

Thirty-pound test monofilament nylon fishing line is the most aesthetically pleasing material to use for suspending herbal baskets.

If plastic baskets are used, their wire hangers can be replaced with the fishing line as well. To help retain moisture in the soil, a plastic basket can be placed inside a moss-covered one—advisable in areas of the United States with high temperatures and winds. However, white or green plastic baskets create a harsh visual effect and in cold climates they retain too much water for successful herb culture. In very hot, windy areas, black plastic sheeting can be cut up and inserted between the moss and soil to help retain moisture. Place drainage holes in the bottom portion of the plastic with a knife or icepick.

With the largest size hanging baskets, three or more pockets can be opened up on the sides for additional plants—which should be young and small. This is also possible using the plastic lining. First wash the roots of the plants to make the root ball small enough for insertion. After the soil is in place in the basket, tease the moss open with your fingers and cut holes in the plastic and insert the plants, one to a pocket. Use a separate piece of wet moss to plug the hole, keeping the plant and soil inside the basket.

Caring for the Plants

IT IS BEST to water hanging herb baskets with a fine spray wand or a watering can with a fine rose on the end. Avoid pouring a rush of water onto the herbs. That will scatter soil, leaving holes and exposing roots. If using a sink or basin filled with water for submerging a basket, be careful about removing the basket suddenly from the water. This can wash away moss and allow some of the soil to escape. If watering in a laundry tub, pull the plug out only one quarter of the way, letting the water out slowly. Rehang the baskets when they are completely drained, as they can be rather heavy right after watering.

Top-dress hanging baskets with a lightweight charcoal to protect the soil from dehydration and to keep the plants clean during rain and waterings.

Hanging baskets should be turned once a week, or even more often, to promote symmetrical growth. Swivel hooks are great for porch ceilings—those with a "security clasp" are safer.

Baskets of herbs can be fertilized just like any other plants. When they are actively growing and their environment is hot, humid, and sunny, plants use up lots of nutrients, so the fertilizer should be increased. Daily watering leaches away a lot of nutrients and makes fertilizing necessary every third or fourth watering. I recommend a 20-20-20 soluble fertilizer unless flower production is desired. Then use a 15-20-15 soluble fertilizer.

Nasturtiums do not need much fertilizer. They will grow many oversized green leaves and few flowers if fertilized—and one wants the flowers for their peppery flavor in salads and sandwiches, and for their decorative effect.

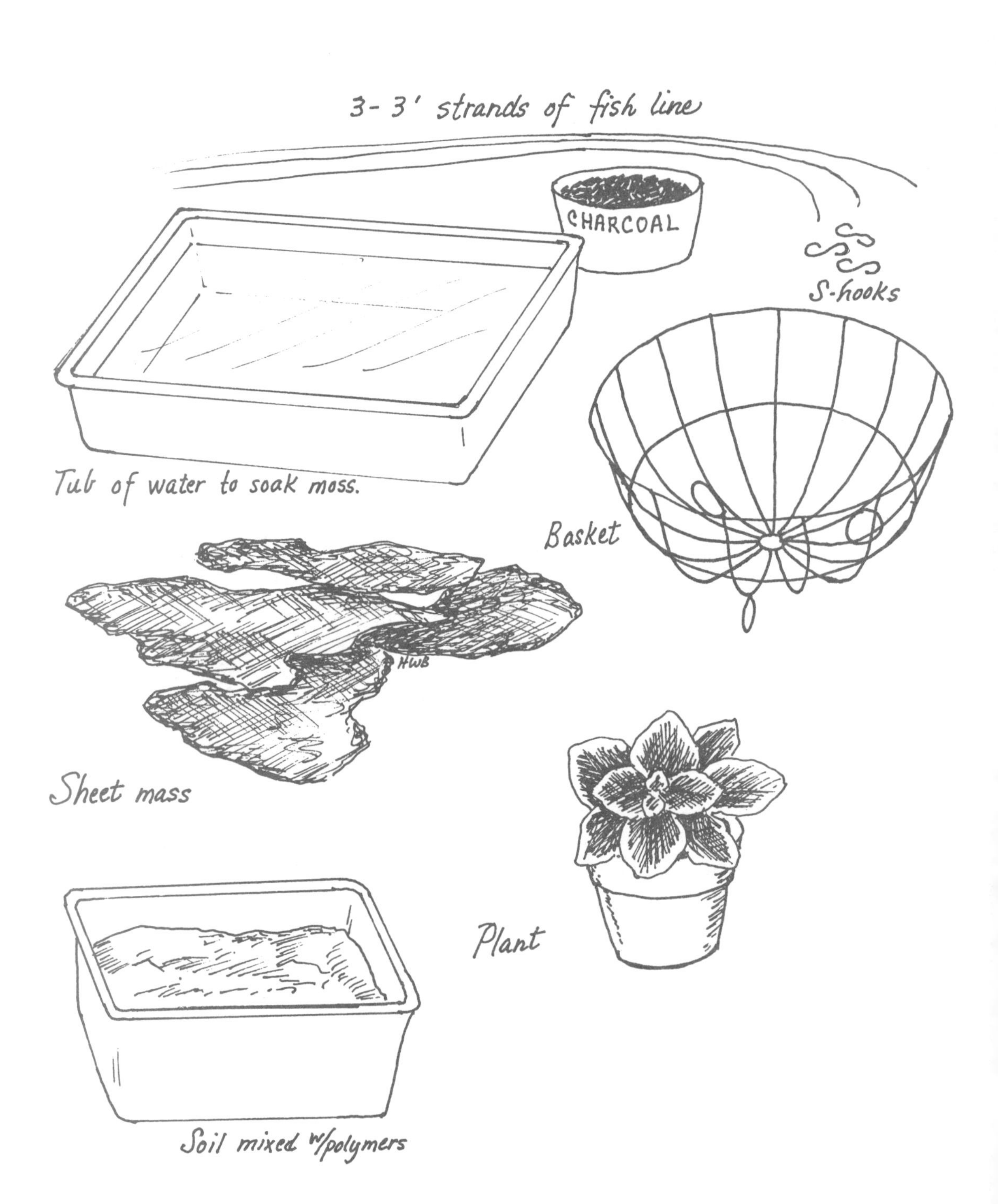
3- 3' strands of fish line
CHARCOAL
S-hooks
Tub of water to soak moss.
Basket
HWB
Sheet mass
Plant
Soil mixed w/polymers

A Plan for Making a Hanging Basket

Assemble the equipment needed:

plant(s)
wire basket (baskets are available from five to fifteen inches in diameter)
two large plastic tubs (one should be filled with water for soaking the moss, another should be dry for mixing the soil and polymers)
sheets of moss
soil
polymers
green carpet thread and needle
charcoal for top dressing
wire or fishing line (30-pound test monofilament), cut into three-foot strands for hanging
shower curtain or "S" hook(s) ("S" hooks come in different sizes. A heavy basket will need three shower curtain hooks pushed together.)
swivel hooks for porches

1. Soak the sheet moss in a tub of water.
2. Using solid sheets, line the basket on the inside with the green part of the moss facing out. Allow one inch of the moss to extend above the rim.
3. Hold the basket up to a light and reinforce the areas where the light shines through. You will require at least two layers of moss.
4. Using green carpet thread and a tapestry needle, secure one end of the thread onto the top wire of the basket with a knot. Then, using a blanket stitch, secure the top one inch of moss to the top loop of wire all the way around the basket to keep the moss from settling below the rim.
5. Center the plant material in the basket. Use a well-drained soil and insert the polymers. Plant high.

6. Top dress with charcoal. This keeps the plant material unsoiled when top watering. Aerial roots can penetrate the charcoal.

7. Wire or nylon fishing line can be used to hang the basket. Wire must be secured tightly with pliers onto the top of the basket at equal intervals. Gather the wires together at the top, braid them, and bend them into a crook. Fishing line can also be tied to the top metal wire of the basket at equal intervals, using either three or four lengths. Nylon is slippery, so tie at least eight knots at the basket end of each strand. Pull hard to tighten the knots. Draw the loose ends together with two or three knots. Then make a loop and tie all six strands together in another knot. Your loop should be three to four inches long. The baskets can be hung from a pipe with shower curtain hooks.

Herbs for Hanging Baskets

Centella asiatica—gotu kola
Colula squalida—bronze buttons (Logee's Greenhouses)
Helichrysum psilolepsis
Lippia dulcis (Phyla scaberrima)—sweet herb (Logee's Greenhouses)
Ocimum basilicum 'Minimum'—bush basil
Ocimum basilicum 'Spicy Globe'—spicy globe basil
Ocimum basilicum 'Purpurascens'—purple bush basil
Origanum dictamnus—Dittany of Crete
Origanum majorana—sweet marjoram
Origanum pulchellum (Logee's Greenhouses)
Origanum vulgare ssp. *hirtum*—Greek oregano, best Italian oregano
Petroselinum crispum 'Crispum'—curly parsley
Plectranthus 'Vick's Vapor Rub'—menthol plant, Vick's vapor plant
Plectranthus amboinicus 'Variegatum'—variegated Spanish thyme
Rosmarinus officinalis 'Blue Boy'—blue boy rosemary
Rosmarinus officinalis 'Prostratus'—prostrate rosemary
Satureja douglasii—yerba buena
Teucrium majoricum (Logee's Greenhouses)
Teucrium marum—cat thyme
Thymbra spicata (Logee's Greenhouses)
Thymus praecox spp. *articus cultivars*—creeping thymes
Tropaeolum majus—nasturtium
Tropaeolum nanum 'Tom Thumb'—dwarf compact nasturtium

HWB
Rosmarinus officinalis
'Lockwoodi de Forest'

CHAPTER 8

Creating a Bonsai with Herbs

HE ANCIENT Eastern art of bonsai has become popular throughout the world. The difference between cultivating bonsai and other container-grown plants is that in bonsai the design of the plant and its harmony with its container are matters of great aesthetic concern.

Colin Ellis expresses well the cultural aspects of bonsai: "In Japan bonsai means a plant or group of plants potted in a container in good balance and harmony, resembling a fully grown plant or plants, but neater (more refined) and more beautiful than the uncultivated plant. . . . The art derives from Taoism, Confucianism and Buddhism in China and from these combined with Shinto in Japan. Each culture has brought its own values. In the West we are beginning to adapt the art to our own culture, since most of us do not have sufficient background in the Eastern cultures." ("The Garden." *Journal of the Royal Horticultural Society,* May 1989.)

Bonsai are designed to represent natural trees, with their trunks and exposed surface roots the major focal point of the composition. In America we can substitute our own familiar plant material for that commonly used in the Orient. We can use woody herbs to create an impression of a

Formal Upright

Informal Upright (Slanting)

Semi Cascade

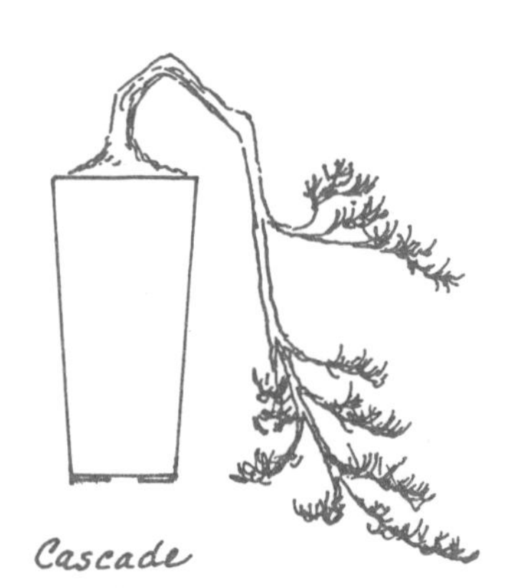

Cascade

mature tree.

When selecting a plant for bonsai consider the shape of the plant's trunk and branches in order to create a bonsai that will be both beautiful and interesting. The branches should accent or complement the trunk line. The scale of bonsai is small and the finished design should resemble a planting in nature.

The planting may be grown in a container or on a stone slab or rock. The roots of the plant need protection and support, and a soil mixture that will provide them with water, food, and air.

The trunks and branches of bonsai are trained by wiring or tying down from the soil surface through the container drainage holes with wire and cords.

Like a topiary, the bonsai must be taken out of its container and root-pruned once a year in order to stimulate the growth of feeder roots, thus renewing the plant itself. New soil is needed to provide the roots with water, nourishment, and oxygen.

Styles of Bonsai

IN GENERAL, bonsai styles fall into seven categories: formal upright, informal upright, slanting, cascade, semicascade, forest, and clump.

For an upright or slanting tree, first select the front of the plant—that side with the most pleasing view of the trunk and its surface roots. A back branch is needed to draw the eye through and to provide depth to the design. Two opposite side branches are also needed but not on the same plane. The lower third of the trunk is kept naked.

The upper branches should alternate, becoming shorter, thinner, and progressively closer together as they march up the trunk. Group several short branches together to form the apex or crown of the tree.

Trim away any leaves or branchlets hiding the trunk and all unwanted branches and dead material.

To achieve the cascade style, one well suited to prostrate rosemary, the trunk should be cultivated to grow upward and then turn downward to reach below the bottom of a deep container. As with the upright and slanting styles, alternating branches on the descending trunk are encouraged, but none should grow on the back side toward the container. This style resembles the effects upon a tree created by a strong wind blowing against it as it grows on an exposed spot on a mountainside.

To start a bonsai one may grow a plant with a single stem from seed or a cutting, or purchase an already growing plant. This plant may be grown on, meaning root-pruned and repotted in a pot one size larger for several years until the trunk at the soil line measures one to four inches. As the plant grows, try to determine the style it suggests—Will it be a straight trunk? A slanting or twisted trunk? A cascading or semicascading style?

A Choice of Herbs

A GOOD SIZED rosemary will make a nice bonsai, as will lavender or santolina, and myrtle. These are the best choices of herbs from which to cultivate bonsai as they are woody plants. Geraniums (another possibility) do not develop truly woody stems. Santolina (lavender cotton) is the most difficult to work with as the centers develop dead leaves and the branches snap easily.

A finished herbal bonsai tree may have only ten or twelve branches. When viewed from above each branch should be triangular in shape, and when viewed from the front the total form should also be a triangle with unequal sides.

Repot your bonsai annually, preferably at the start of the growing season. Top-pruning can be done at the same time, but not wiring. One should do only two of these three procedures at one time.

Some professionals prune and wire bonsai prior to potting. Others pot or repot first then rest the plant for several weeks before wiring and pruning.

The principles and styles of bonsai are covered in many specialized books. Recommended to the reader is the Time-Life Encyclopedia of Gardening, *Miniatures and Bonsai* (New York: Time-Life Books, 1972), which features good text and drawings.

General Procedures for Creating a Bonsai with Herbs

1. Decide on the desired style and eventual shape of the bonsai.

2. Select the herbs to be used (woody plants are best).

3. Transfer the plant from a standard container to a bulb pot, adding bonsai soil. In transferring, root-prune but make sure that those roots left are radiated evenly over a hill of soil.

Water when dry, fertilize once a month, and continue shaping the trunk and branches of the plant.

Transfer into a bonsai container the following spring, after one growing season in the bulb pan.

A Note about Containers: Bonsai containers should be shallow for upright styles and deep for cascading styles. Design and decoration should be strongly angular for heavy trees and lighter, more curving and decorative for light trees. The material can be glazed or unglazed, but the color of the container should be muted. The goal is to contrast or complement some aspect of the tree—its bark, leaves, flowers, or fruit color.

4. Transfer the plant from the bulb pan to a bonsai container.

Cover drainage holes with plastic window screening. Wire each piece of screening into place using a loop of wire with edges secured onto the bottom of the container.

Remove enough soil and roots from the plant so that what remains will take up sixty percent of the container. Add bonsai soil, using a chopstick to tamp and push soil around the roots.

Wire the entire plant into the container from soil level through the drainage holes.

Bottom water by placing the container in a pan or sink with the water level just below the lip of the pot.

Water from the top using a fine spray.

5. Remove all unwanted plant material—dead, weak, or crossing branches—and thin the major branches, opening up the plant.

6. Train the trunk and branches. Training is best done on a dry plant, which is easier to bend.

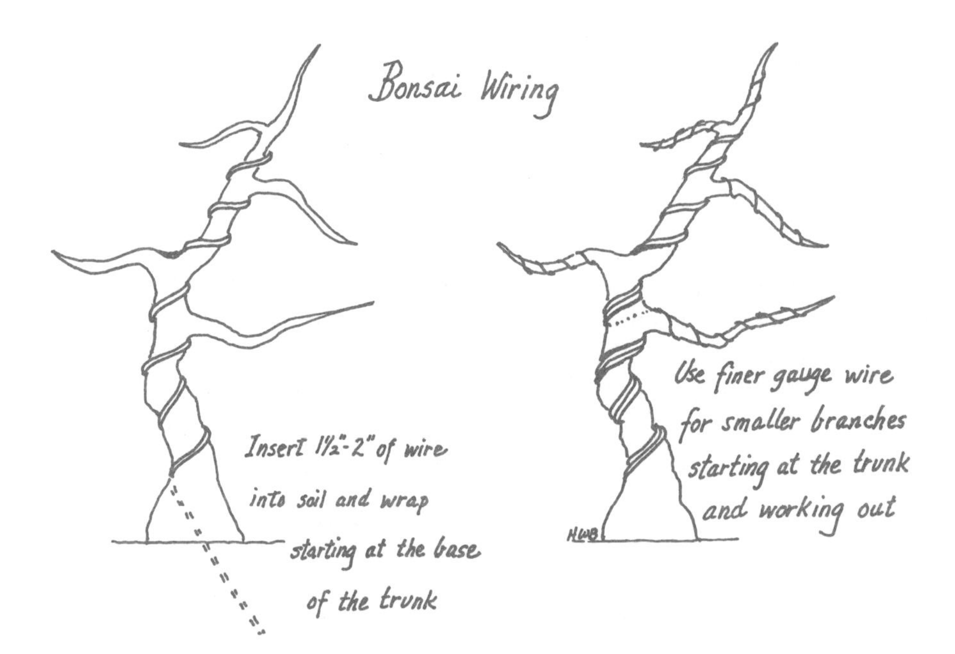

45°

Angle of wiring
should be 45 degrees

For more strength, use 2 or 3 wires:
Wrap one at a time ~ Follow
closely with the second maintaining
the same angle. Likewise for a third.

Cut wire on back side
of branch
before reaching the
end of a small branch

About Wire-Types and Techniques

USE WIRE of different gauges—heaviest for the trunk, lightest for the branchlets. (Wire gauges run from #4 to #26.)

Cord can be used to tie down the branches instead of wire. Fasten the cords into the container through the drainage holes.

Both wire and cord can be used in training, particularly for the lower branches.

Types of wire

Copper must be annealed to make it more flexible before it is used in training. Using a gas burner or barbecue grill, heat the wire to a red glow. Allow to cool before touching or removing it from the burner or grill—cooling takes time.

Aluminum wire does not need to be annealed. Buy aluminum wire that has a dull copper-like finish.

Wire technique

Wire only those trunks and branches that require a change in the direction of their growth. For the trunk, anchor wire one third the diameter of the trunk into the soil. (Two or three pieces are sometimes needed—they are put on separately but work together as one.) Wrap the wire around the trunk at a 45 degree angle—not too snugly, allowing room for growth—in bands approximately one-half inch apart, according to the size of the trunk. If using aluminum wire, it should be one-half the diameter of the trunk.

Work from the thickest branch and wire systematically to the thinnest, using different wires as needed.

Bend the wired branch into the desired shape using your thumbs as support.

Removing wire

When the desired form of the bonsai is set (usually after one growing season) remove any wires. On a branch where the wire has indented the bark, rewiring may be necessary as the branch did not set into the desired position. Rewire in the opposite direction.

Remove wires with special wire cutters, cutting every inch so that the wires fall off. Do not cut the bark.

Wire should also be removed when it is cutting into the bark.

Bonsai Soil

two parts Terra-Green
one part leaf mold put through a ¼ inch sieve
slow release fertilizer pellets (such as Osmocote 14-14-14), ¼ cup to one quart of soil

Appropriate Herbs for Bonsai

Cuphea hyssopifolia—elfin herb, false heather
Myrtus communis 'Microphylla'—dwarf myrtle, German myrtle
Rosmarinus officinalis—rosemary
Rosmarinus officinalis 'Prostratus'—prostrate rosemary

CHAPTER 9

Propagation of Ornamental Herbs

GARDENERS commonly raise annuals and biennials from seed. Growing from seed is not only exciting and great fun but humbling. To start with a seed the size of a grain of pepper and in a year or two have a plant several feet in diameter is indeed a miraculous process to behold.

Once a dry seed is moistened the outer seed coat will start to absorb water. When 12 percent of a seed's total bulk is water, the seed will start to germinate and growth will begin. Seed once planted must never be allowed to become dry.

It is a well known horticultural fact that there can be great variation in seedlings. When growing herbs for ornamental purposes the more compact the plant is the better. Hybrid plants and most horticultural varieties do not breed true from seed. Often seedlings do not retain the best characteristics of the parents.

Division and cuttings of certain plants are surer methods of propagation that almost always result in progeny identical with the parent plant.

rubber band
Seed pan with identifying label (sandwich bag covering top)
Prick out seedling ~
Transfer to individual pot
Pot on to larger pots as plant grows

Sowing Herb Seed

I SOW ALL my annual herb seeds in dry Metromix #360 in small plastic pans 2″ × 2″ × 3″ deep. I place a piece of torn paper towel in the bottom of the pans, covering the seeds with this same mixture to the depth of the thickness of the seed. I label each pan with both botanical and common names, the source of the seed, and the date it was sown. I use a 4-inch label and a Pilot pen with an ultra-fine point and permanent ink. I do not use all the seed in the envelope unless it comes from the Royal Horticultural Society. They distribute to a membership numbering over 100,000 and one is lucky to receive even a few seeds. As it arrives by mail I place the seed inside a tin can, with a tight lid, in the refrigerator until ready to plant. (Seeds can be successfully stored there.)

As soon as the seed is sown I place the pan in a sink of water about one- to two-inches deep. When the soil is moist, I remove each pan, drain it, and slip a plastic sandwich bag (the thinnest kind) over the entire pan, including the label. I keep a rubber band around the waist of the pan to hold the plastic bag in place. Then I set the pan in very bright light on bottom heat of 70° F. I check the pans every day, opening the bags to look for anything green. As soon as the seedlings appear I remove the bag for good. I keep fans going and have good air circulation. All this takes place in my greenhouse on a wooden bench with no shading from the early spring sun, which is still low in the sky. While night temperatures are usually 55° F, the heatpad stays at 70° F.

These seed pans are kept moist, and I always bottom water in the sink. Once a week I add a small amount of fertilizer to the water even though there is already a small amount of fertilizer in the Metromix. When the seedlings have developed their first true leaves I prick the plants out into wooden flats (5″ × 8″ × 3½″ deep), plastic pots, or six packs—whatever is handy and appropriate for the plant. I use paper towels to keep the soil from running out the drainage holes. Then I place the seedlings on a bench in bright light and mark each container or pot with an individual label made up ahead of time.

Be careful not to overpot. A tiny seedling will not occupy a space more than 2″ × 2″ × 3″ deep. Often I have to pot on a second or third time into the next size container prior to using these plants or sending them off to be sold. With too much soil around a set of roots, a plant rots.

Actually, I use Metromix #350 or #360 for all sowing, pricking out and potting on. For young herbs going into the garden, I switch to

Potting on –
Salvia officinalis

homemade soil—one part perlite, one part compost (put through a quarter-inch sieve), and one part Canadian sphagnum peat (also put through a quarter-inch sieve). The peat must be moistened with hot water after going through the sieve and prior to using it in the soil mix.

I often supply plants to our local unit of the Herb Society of America herb sale. The number and types of herbs are decided ahead of time, according to present demand and what has sold well previously. I recommend sharing plants with other people. It is very satisfying and serves as a way of introducing interesting varieties of plants to others. Growers love the surprise that comes from growing a new and interesting plant.

By the time these plants go into the garden or into strawberry jars and window boxes, they have been hardened off—that is, they go outside during the day and inside the greenhouse at night.

If the herb seeds are to be started indoors it is best to place them under lights (one cool and one warm fluorescent bulb), on a sixteen-hour day about four inches from the light source. As the seedlings grow, raise the lights to maintain a four- to six-inch clearance.

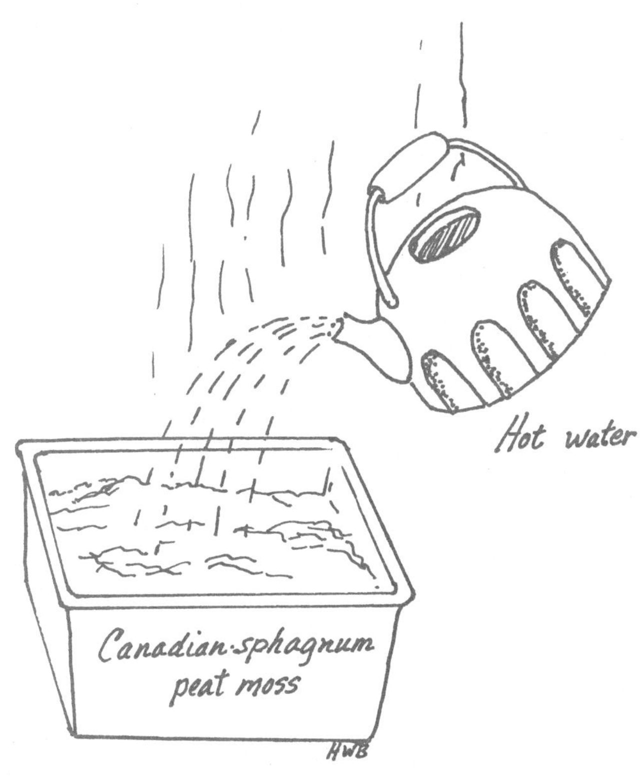

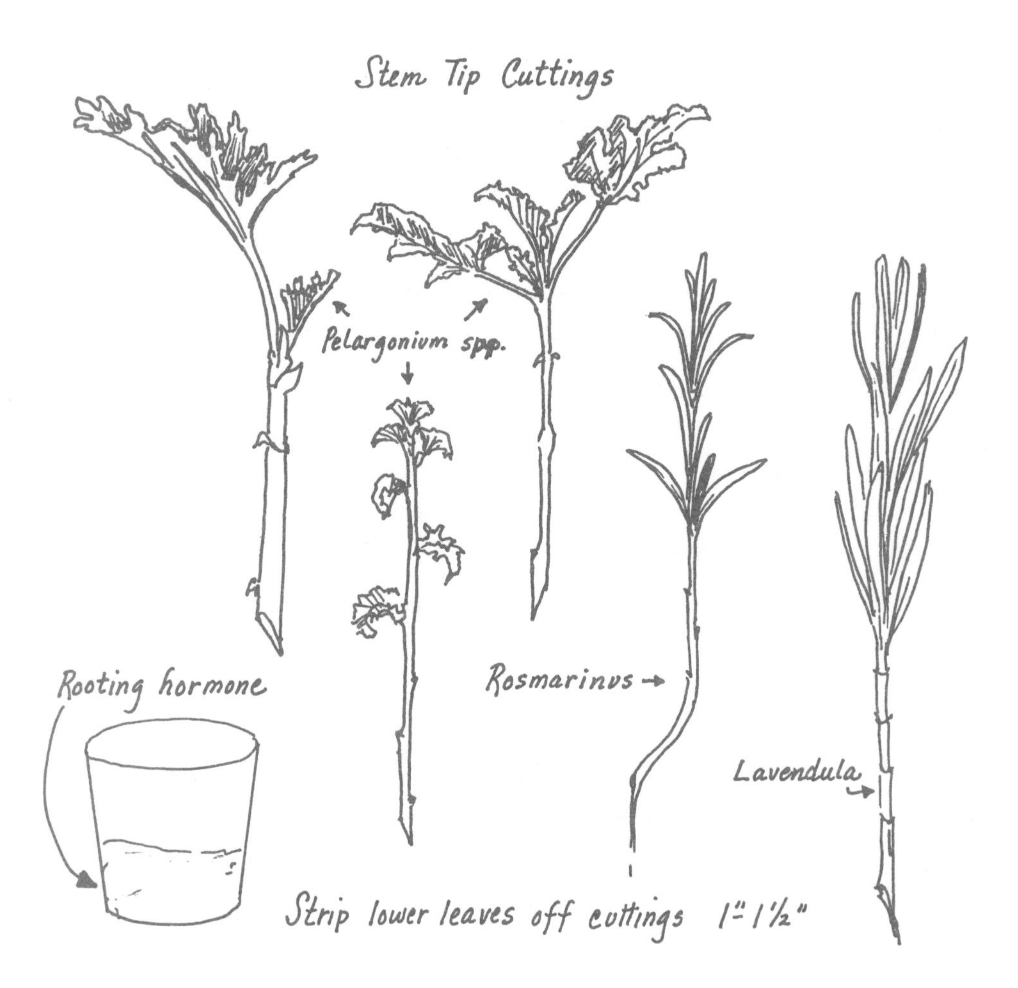
Stem Tip Cuttings
Pelargonium spp.
Rooting hormone
Rosmarinus
Lavendula
Strip lower leaves off cuttings 1"-1½"

Indoors, herb seeds should be started three months before the last frost date if the plants are to summer outside. Basil should be sown last, as it is the most sensitive to cold. Herbs for indoor winter growing should be started from seed one month before the fall frost date. For a kitchen winter windowsill of herbs I suggest starting from seed: basil, chervil, coriander, dill, summer savory, thyme, marjoram, and parsley. Start sage from a cutting and chives from division.

Starting Herbs from Cuttings

HERBS CAN ALSO be started from cuttings. In my greenhouse I keep a plastic pan filled with large-sized perlite which is replenished when needed. A heating cable runs through the pan; the heat is disconnected during the warm months. Into the perlite go cuttings from my herbal topiaries and from perennial herbs that were in my strawberry jars all summer. Before placing the cuttings in perlite, I strip all leaves 1 to 1½ inches from the bottom of the stem. I use rooting hormone sparingly and shake off the excess before inserting the cuttings into the perlite. Cleanliness is very important in preventing diseases from forming in the fresh wounds. This means washing one's hands well, disinfecting the instruments used, and cleansing the bench or surface where the cuttings sit before insertion. Geranium cuttings should sit fifteen minutes to form a callus before being inserted in rooting hormone and perlite. If one roots only scented-leaf geraniums, a mixture of peat and perlite is a good rooting medium.

Cuttings take from two weeks to several months to root over winter. I pot them when I can tug the stem and find resistance. The same cuttings pan can go into the house under lights, heating cable included. Indoors, however, a plastic covering is needed to maintain the proper humidity. I water the large-sized perlite every few days. Each cutting is labeled and the sun shines on the pan briefly as it is filtered by hanging baskets.

I grow the sages, lavenders, rosemaries, geraniums, and bay (which can take up to one year to root) from cuttings. The hardy herbs—chives, French tarragon, and the mints (excepting pennyroyal and Corsican mint, which in our Zone 5 are not hardy)—I divide in early spring into clumps of three- to four-inches in diameter. German chamomile and sometimes dill self-sow in the garden. (Pennyroyal and Corsican mint I restart from seed.)

I pinch out the centers of my rooted cuttings when they reach three to four inches in height, unless they are to be used for standards or a tied topiary where I need a straight central leader. The latter I start training when they reach five to six inches in height.

Defining Terms

IT MAY BE HELPFUL at this point to define the terms *annual, biennial,* and *perennial.*

An *annual* is any plant that can be sown from seed and that will mature in a single growing season to flower and seed. It completes its life cycle in one season.

A *biennial* takes two years to complete its life cycle. The first year it grows roots, stems, and leaves. The second year, having died to the ground during winter's cold, it sends up all of the above and then flowers, sets seeds, and dies.

A *perennial* is a plant that endures winter cold and comes back from its roots each season to send up shoots and eventually flowers and seeds. A tender perennial is a plant which is marginally hardy in one's geographical location. (It is possible to pull it through a winter if well mulched.)

Herbs to Grow from Seed	***Type***
Aloysia triphylla—lemon verbena	tender, shrubby perennial
Anethum graveolens—dill	annual
Anthriscus cerefolium—chervil	biennial
Carum carvi—caraway	biennial
Centella asiatica—gotu kola	perennial
Chamaemelum nobile—chamomile	annual, North; perennial, South
Coriandrum sativum—coriander, cilantro	annual
Cuphea hyssopifolia—elfin herb	tender shrub
Mentha pulegium—pennyroyal	tender perennial, North
Mentha requienii—Corsican mint	perennial, South
Ocimum spp.—basil	annual
Origanum majorana—sweet marjoram	annual
Petroselinum spp.—parsley	biennial
Santolina chamaecyparissus—lavender cotton	tender, shrubby perennial
Satureja spp.—savory	annual, North
Thymus spp.—thyme	perennial
Tropaeolum majus—nasturtium	annual

Herbs to Grow from Stem Tip Cuttings	***Type***
Aloysia triphylla—lemon verbena	tender, shrubby perennial
Artemisia dracunculus 'Sativa'—French tarragon	perennial
Helichrysum spp. (the silver ones)	tender perennial
Laurus nobilis—sweet bay	tender, shrubby perennial
Lavandula spp—Lavenders	tender, shrubby perennial
Leptospermum scoparium—New Zealand tea tree	tender, shrubby perennial
Lippia dulcis—sweet herb	tender, shrubby perennial
Myrtus spp.—myrtle	tender, shrubby perennial
Origanum vulgare spp. *hirtum*—Greek oregano	tender perennial (hardy to 0° F)

Origanum dictamnus—Dittany of Crete	tender perennial (hardy to 0° F)
Pelargonium spp.—scented-leaf geraniums	tender perennial
Rosmarinus spp.—rosemary	tender, shrubby perennial
Salvia spp.—sage	tender, shrubby perennial
Santolina spp.—santolina, lavender cotton	tender, shrubby perennial
Satureja spp.—savory	shrubby perennial
Teucrium spp.—germander	tender, shrubby perennial
Thymbra spicata	tender, shrubby perennial
Thymus spp.—thyme	tender, shrubby perennial

Herbs to Grow by Division	***Type***
Allium schoenoprasum—chives	perennial
Artemesia dracunculus 'Sativa'—French tarragon	perennial
Cotula squalida—bronze buttons	tender perennial
Mentha spp.—mint	perennial
Thymus spp.—thyme	perennial

Herbs to Grow from Offsets/Runners

Cantella asiatica—gotu kola	perennial

Ornamental Herbs Arranged by Families

Compositae

Artemisia dracunculus
Chamaemelum nobile
Cotula squalida
Helichrysum spp.
Santolina spp.

Geraniaceae

Pelargonium spp.

Labiatae

Lavandula spp.
Mentha pulegium
Mentha requienii
Ocimum spp.
Origanum spp.
Plectranthus spp.
Rosmarinus spp.
Salvia spp.
Satureja spp.
Teucruim spp.
Thymbra spicata
Thymus spp.

Lauraceae

Laurus nobilis

Liliaceae

Allium schoenoprasum

Lythraceae

Cuphea hyssopifolia

Myrtaceae

Leptospermum scoparium
Myrtus spp.

Tropaeolaceae

Tropaeolum spp.

Verbenaceae

Aloysia triphylla
Lippia dulcis

Umbelliferae

Anethum graveolens
Anthriscus cerefolium
Carum carvi
Centella asiatica
Coriandrum sativum
Petroselinum spp.

*Sources of Seeds, Plants, and Supplies**

There may be adequate sources nearer than these to some readers' locations. The ones mentioned here are those I have patronized and believe to be reliable.

Aquatrols Corp of America
1432 Union Avenue
Pennsauken, NJ 08110
(800) 257-7797
—Polymers called SuperSorb C

Bio-Control Co.
Box 337
Berry Creek, CA 95916
(916) 589-5227
—lady beetles (lady bugs)
—will ship

Brookstone Hard to Find Tools
127 Vose Farm Road
Peterborough, NH 03458
(603) 924-9541
—items available: fans and instruments; small portable uncaged fans (#M-04418)
—94 stores nationwide
—write for a free catalog
—will ship

Caprilands Herb Farm
Silver Street
Coventry, CT 06238
(203) 742-7244
—specializes in herb plants
—send self-addressed, stamped envelope for a free catalog
—will ship

Charcoal Supply Co.
1186 North Cherry Avenue
Chicago, IL 60622
(312) MI2-5538
—I recommend their "Horticultural Charcoal," grade #3 (available in 25 lb and 50 lb bags).
—will ship

Fox Hill Farm
444 W. Michigan Avenue, Box 9
Parma, MI 49269-009
(517) 531-3179
—herbs, fragrant plants, and herbal foods
—shopping list is free
—will ship

Florist Products, Inc.
2242 North Palmer Drive
Schaumburg, IL 60173
(800) 828-2242
—Items available: sheet moss; polymers; Grace's Metromix #350, #360; 14-gauge (0.08") green wire stakes, in lengths of 12", 18", 24", 1,000 per bundle; 8-gauge (0.162") galvanized metal Rose Stakes in lengths of 36", 48", 72", 100 per bundle; and most products mentioned in this book
—write or call for a free catalog
—will ship

Logee's Greenhouses
55 North Street
Danielson, CT 06239
(203) 774-8039
—specialize in rare herb plants and scented geraniums
—catalog $3.00
—will ship

Oil Dri Corp. of America
520 North Michigan Avenue
Chicago, IL 60611
(312) 321-1515
—Terra-Green, available in three mesh sizes
—I recommend their "Soil Conditioner"

Richter's
Box 26
Goodwod, Ontario, Canada IAO
(414) 640-6677
—specializes in herb seeds and plants
—catalog $1.00
—will ship

Sunnybrook Farms and Nursery
Box 6
9448 Mayfield Road
Chesterland, OH 44026
(216) 729-7232
—specializes in herb plants and scented geraniums
—catalog $1.00
—will ship

T. DeBaggio Herbs Mail Order
923 North Ivy Street
Arlington, VA 22201
(703) 243-2498
—developer of new varieties
—extensive list of rosemary and lavender varieties
—catalog $1.00

Topiary, Inc.
41 Bering Street
Tampa, FL 33606
(813) 254-3229
—will do custom-ordered designs
—send self-addressed, stamped envelope for an illustrated list of galvanized metal frames
—will ship

Unique Insect Control
Box 15376
Sacramento, CA 95851
(916) 961-7945
—lady beetles (lady bugs)

Vine Arts
Janet Schuster
Box 83014
Portland, OR 97283-0014
(503) 289-7505
—galvanized wire topiary frames available
—send self-addressed, stamped envelope for an illustrated price list
—will ship

Well-Sweep Herb Farms
317 Mt. Bethel Road
Port Murray, NJ 07865
(201) 852-5390
—specialize in herb plants
—offer over 40 varieties of rosemary
—catalog $1.00
—will ship

*The following items can most likely be found at any local garden center: Gibberellic Acid; Metromix #350 or #360; Peters Professional Potting Soil; polymers; Safer's Soap; soil wetting agent; Sunshine All-Purpose Potting Mix; and Wilt-Pruf.